Samurai: A Very Short Introduction

VERY SHORT INTRODUCTIONS are for anyone wanting a stimulating and accessible way into a new subject. They are written by experts, and have been translated into more than 45 different languages.

The series began in 1995, and now covers a wide variety of topics in every discipline. The VSI library currently contains over 550 volumes—a Very Short Introduction to everything from Psychology and Philosophy of Science to American History and Relativity—and continues to grow in every subject area.

Very Short Introductions available now:

ABOLITIONISM Richard S. Newman
THE ABRAHAMIC RELIGIONS Charles L. Cohen
ACCOUNTING Christopher Nobes
ADAM SMITH Christopher J. Berry
ADOLESCENCE Peter K. Smith
ADVERTISING Winston Fletcher
AERIAL WARFARE Frank Ledwidge
AESTHETICS Bence Nanay
AFRICAN AMERICAN RELIGION Eddie S. Glaude Jr
AFRICAN HISTORY John Parker and Richard Rathbone
AFRICAN POLITICS Ian Taylor
AFRICAN RELIGIONS Jacob K. Olupona
AGEING Nancy A. Pachana
AGNOSTICISM Robin Le Poidevin
AGRICULTURE Paul Brassley and Richard Soffe
ALBERT CAMUS Oliver Gloag
ALEXANDER THE GREAT Hugh Bowden
ALGEBRA Peter M. Higgins
AMERICAN BUSINESS HISTORY Walter A. Friedman
AMERICAN CULTURAL HISTORY Eric Avila
AMERICAN FOREIGN RELATIONS Andrew Preston
AMERICAN HISTORY Paul S. Boyer
AMERICAN IMMIGRATION David A. Gerber
AMERICAN LEGAL HISTORY G. Edward White
AMERICAN MILITARY HISTORY Joseph T. Glatthaar
AMERICAN NAVAL HISTORY Craig L. Symonds
AMERICAN POLITICAL HISTORY Donald Critchlow
AMERICAN POLITICAL PARTIES AND ELECTIONS L. Sandy Maisel
AMERICAN POLITICS Richard M. Valelly
THE AMERICAN PRESIDENCY Charles O. Jones
THE AMERICAN REVOLUTION Robert J. Allison
AMERICAN SLAVERY Heather Andrea Williams
THE AMERICAN SOUTH Charles Reagan Wilson
THE AMERICAN WEST Stephen Aron
AMERICAN WOMEN'S HISTORY Susan Ware
AMPHIBIANS T. S. Kemp
ANAESTHESIA Aidan O'Donnell
ANALYTIC PHILOSOPHY Michael Beaney
ANARCHISM Colin Ward
ANCIENT ASSYRIA Karen Radner
ANCIENT EGYPT Ian Shaw
ANCIENT EGYPTIAN ART AND ARCHITECTURE Christina Riggs
ANCIENT GREECE Paul Cartledge
THE ANCIENT NEAR EAST Amanda H. Podany
ANCIENT PHILOSOPHY Julia Annas

ANCIENT WARFARE Harry Sidebottom
ANGELS David Albert Jones
ANGLICANISM Mark Chapman
THE ANGLO-SAXON AGE John Blair
ANIMAL BEHAVIOUR
Tristram D. Wyatt
THE ANIMAL KINGDOM
Peter Holland
ANIMAL RIGHTS David DeGrazia
THE ANTARCTIC Klaus Dodds
ANTHROPOCENE Erle C. Ellis
ANTISEMITISM Steven Beller
ANXIETY Daniel Freeman and
Jason Freeman
THE APOCRYPHAL GOSPELS
Paul Foster
APPLIED MATHEMATICS
Alain Goriely
ARBITRATION Thomas Schultz and
Thomas Grant
ARCHAEOLOGY Paul Bahn
ARCHITECTURE Andrew Ballantyne
ARISTOCRACY William Doyle
ARISTOTLE Jonathan Barnes
ART HISTORY Dana Arnold
ART THEORY Cynthia Freeland
ARTIFICIAL INTELLIGENCE
Margaret A. Boden
ASIAN AMERICAN HISTORY
Madeline Y. Hsu
ASTROBIOLOGY David C. Catling
ASTROPHYSICS James Binney
ATHEISM Julian Baggini
THE ATMOSPHERE Paul I. Palmer
AUGUSTINE Henry Chadwick
AUSTRALIA Kenneth Morgan
AUTISM Uta Frith
AUTOBIOGRAPHY Laura Marcus
THE AVANT GARDE David Cottington
THE AZTECS Davíd Carrasco
BABYLONIA Trevor Bryce
BACTERIA Sebastian G. B. Amyes
BANKING John Goddard and
John O. S. Wilson
BARTHES Jonathan Culler
THE BEATS David Sterritt
BEAUTY Roger Scruton
BEHAVIOURAL ECONOMICS
Michelle Baddeley
BESTSELLERS John Sutherland
THE BIBLE John Riches
BIBLICAL ARCHAEOLOGY
Eric H. Cline
BIG DATA Dawn E. Holmes
BIOCHEMISTRY Mark Lorch
BIOGEOGRAPHY Mark V. Lomolino
BIOGRAPHY Hermione Lee
BIOMETRICS Michael Fairhurst
BLACK HOLES Katherine Blundell
BLOOD Chris Cooper
THE BLUES Elijah Wald
THE BODY Chris Shilling
THE BOOK OF COMMON
PRAYER Brian Cummings
THE BOOK OF MORMON
Terryl Givens
BORDERS Alexander C. Diener and
Joshua Hagen
THE BRAIN Michael O'Shea
BRANDING Robert Jones
THE BRICS Andrew F. Cooper
THE BRITISH CONSTITUTION
Martin Loughlin
THE BRITISH EMPIRE Ashley Jackson
BRITISH POLITICS Tony Wright
BUDDHA Michael Carrithers
BUDDHISM Damien Keown
BUDDHIST ETHICS Damien Keown
BYZANTIUM Peter Sarris
C. S. LEWIS James Como
CALVINISM Jon Balserak
CANADA Donald Wright
CANCER Nicholas James
CAPITALISM James Fulcher
CATHOLICISM Gerald O'Collins
CAUSATION Stephen Mumford and
Rani Lill Anjum
THE CELL Terence Allen and
Graham Cowling
THE CELTS Barry Cunliffe
CHAOS Leonard Smith
CHARLES DICKENS Jenny Hartley
CHEMISTRY Peter Atkins
CHILD PSYCHOLOGY Usha Goswami
CHILDREN'S LITERATURE
Kimberley Reynolds
CHINESE LITERATURE
Sabina Knight
CHOICE THEORY Michael Allingham
CHRISTIAN ART Beth Williamson
CHRISTIAN ETHICS D. Stephen Long
CHRISTIANITY Linda Woodhead

CIRCADIAN RHYTHMS Russell Foster and Leon Kreitzman
CITIZENSHIP Richard Bellamy
CITY PLANNING Carl Abbott
CIVIL ENGINEERING David Muir Wood
CLASSICAL LITERATURE William Allan
CLASSICAL MYTHOLOGY Helen Morales
CLASSICS Mary Beard and John Henderson
CLAUSEWITZ Michael Howard
CLIMATE Mark Maslin
CLIMATE CHANGE Mark Maslin
CLINICAL PSYCHOLOGY Susan Llewelyn and Katie Aafjes-van Doorn
COGNITIVE NEUROSCIENCE Richard Passingham
THE COLD WAR Robert J. McMahon
COLONIAL AMERICA Alan Taylor
COLONIAL LATIN AMERICAN LITERATURE Rolena Adorno
COMBINATORICS Robin Wilson
COMEDY Matthew Bevis
COMMUNISM Leslie Holmes
COMPARATIVE LITERATURE Ben Hutchinson
COMPLEXITY John H. Holland
THE COMPUTER Darrel Ince
COMPUTER SCIENCE Subrata Dasgupta
CONCENTRATION CAMPS Dan Stone
CONFUCIANISM Daniel K. Gardner
THE CONQUISTADORS Matthew Restall and Felipe Fernández-Armesto
CONSCIENCE Paul Strohm
CONSCIOUSNESS Susan Blackmore
CONTEMPORARY ART Julian Stallabrass
CONTEMPORARY FICTION Robert Eaglestone
CONTINENTAL PHILOSOPHY Simon Critchley
COPERNICUS Owen Gingerich
CORAL REEFS Charles Sheppard
CORPORATE SOCIAL RESPONSIBILITY Jeremy Moon
CORRUPTION Leslie Holmes
COSMOLOGY Peter Coles
COUNTRY MUSIC Richard Carlin
CREATIVITY Vlad Glăveanu
CRIME FICTION Richard Bradford
CRIMINAL JUSTICE Julian V. Roberts
CRIMINOLOGY Tim Newburn
CRITICAL THEORY Stephen Eric Bronner
THE CRUSADES Christopher Tyerman
CRYPTOGRAPHY Fred Piper and Sean Murphy
CRYSTALLOGRAPHY A. M. Glazer
THE CULTURAL REVOLUTION Richard Curt Kraus
DADA AND SURREALISM David Hopkins
DANTE Peter Hainsworth and David Robey
DARWIN Jonathan Howard
THE DEAD SEA SCROLLS Timothy H. Lim
DECADENCE David Weir
DECOLONIZATION Dane Kennedy
DEMENTIA Kathleen Taylor
DEMOCRACY Bernard Crick
DEMOGRAPHY Sarah Harper
DEPRESSION Jan Scott and Mary Jane Tacchi
DERRIDA Simon Glendinning
DESCARTES Tom Sorell
DESERTS Nick Middleton
DESIGN John Heskett
DEVELOPMENT Ian Goldin
DEVELOPMENTAL BIOLOGY Lewis Wolpert
THE DEVIL Darren Oldridge
DIASPORA Kevin Kenny
DICTIONARIES Lynda Mugglestone
DINOSAURS David Norman
DIPLOMACY Joseph M. Siracusa
DOCUMENTARY FILM Patricia Aufderheide
DREAMING J. Allan Hobson
DRUGS Les Iversen
DRUIDS Barry Cunliffe
DYNASTY Jeroen Duindam
DYSLEXIA Margaret J. Snowling
EARLY MUSIC Thomas Forrest Kelly
THE EARTH Martin Redfern
EARTH SYSTEM SCIENCE Tim Lenton
ECOLOGY Jaboury Ghazoul
ECONOMICS Partha Dasgupta
EDUCATION Gary Thomas
EGYPTIAN MYTH Geraldine Pinch

EIGHTEENTH-CENTURY BRITAIN Paul Langford
THE ELEMENTS Philip Ball
ÉMILE ZOLA Brian Nelson
EMOTION Dylan Evans
EMPIRE Stephen Howe
ENERGY SYSTEMS Nick Jenkins
ENGELS Terrell Carver
ENGINEERING David Blockley
THE ENGLISH LANGUAGE Simon Horobin
ENGLISH LITERATURE Jonathan Bate
THE ENLIGHTENMENT John Robertson
ENTREPRENEURSHIP Paul Westhead and Mike Wright
ENVIRONMENTAL ECONOMICS Stephen Smith
ENVIRONMENTAL ETHICS Robin Attfield
ENVIRONMENTAL LAW Elizabeth Fisher
ENVIRONMENTAL POLITICS Andrew Dobson
ENZYMES Paul Engel
EPICUREANISM Catherine Wilson
EPIDEMIOLOGY Rodolfo Saracci
ETHICS Simon Blackburn
ETHNOMUSICOLOGY Timothy Rice
THE ETRUSCANS Christopher Smith
EUGENICS Philippa Levine
THE EUROPEAN UNION Simon Usherwood and John Pinder
EUROPEAN UNION LAW Anthony Arnull
EVOLUTION Brian and Deborah Charlesworth
EXISTENTIALISM Thomas Flynn
EXPLORATION Stewart A. Weaver
EXTINCTION Paul B. Wignall
THE EYE Michael Land
FAIRY TALE Marina Warner
FAMILY LAW Jonathan Herring
FASCISM Kevin Passmore
FASHION Rebecca Arnold
FEDERALISM Mark J. Rozell and Clyde Wilcox
FEMINISM Margaret Walters
FILM Michael Wood
FILM MUSIC Kathryn Kalinak
FILM NOIR James Naremore
FIRE Andrew C. Scott
THE FIRST WORLD WAR Michael Howard
FOLK MUSIC Mark Slobin
FOOD John Krebs
FORENSIC PSYCHOLOGY David Canter
FORENSIC SCIENCE Jim Fraser
FORESTS Jaboury Ghazoul
FOSSILS Keith Thomson
FOUCAULT Gary Gutting
THE FOUNDING FATHERS R. B. Bernstein
FRACTALS Kenneth Falconer
FREE SPEECH Nigel Warburton
FREE WILL Thomas Pink
FREEMASONRY Andreas Önnerfors
FRENCH LITERATURE John D. Lyons
FRENCH PHILOSOPHY Stephen Gaukroger and Knox Peden
THE FRENCH REVOLUTION William Doyle
FREUD Anthony Storr
FUNDAMENTALISM Malise Ruthven
FUNGI Nicholas P. Money
THE FUTURE Jennifer M. Gidley
GALAXIES John Gribbin
GALILEO Stillman Drake
GAME THEORY Ken Binmore
GANDHI Bhikhu Parekh
GARDEN HISTORY Gordon Campbell
GENES Jonathan Slack
GENIUS Andrew Robinson
GENOMICS John Archibald
GEOFFREY CHAUCER David Wallace
GEOGRAPHY John Matthews and David Herbert
GEOLOGY Jan Zalasiewicz
GEOPHYSICS William Lowrie
GEOPOLITICS Klaus Dodds
GEORGE BERNARD SHAW Christopher Wixson
GERMAN LITERATURE Nicholas Boyle
GERMAN PHILOSOPHY Andrew Bowie
THE GHETTO Bryan Cheyette
GLACIATION David J. A. Evans
GLOBAL CATASTROPHES Bill McGuire
GLOBAL ECONOMIC HISTORY Robert C. Allen
GLOBAL ISLAM Nile Green

GLOBALIZATION Manfred B. Steger
GOD John Bowker
GOETHE Ritchie Robertson
THE GOTHIC Nick Groom
GOVERNANCE Mark Bevir
GRAVITY Timothy Clifton
THE GREAT DEPRESSION AND THE NEW DEAL Eric Rauchway
HABERMAS James Gordon Finlayson
THE HABSBURG EMPIRE Martyn Rady
HAPPINESS Daniel M. Haybron
THE HARLEM RENAISSANCE Cheryl A. Wall
THE HEBREW BIBLE AS LITERATURE Tod Linafelt
HEGEL Peter Singer
HEIDEGGER Michael Inwood
THE HELLENISTIC AGE Peter Thonemann
HEREDITY John Waller
HERMENEUTICS Jens Zimmermann
HERODOTUS Jennifer T. Roberts
HIEROGLYPHS Penelope Wilson
HINDUISM Kim Knott
HISTORY John H. Arnold
THE HISTORY OF ASTRONOMY Michael Hoskin
THE HISTORY OF CHEMISTRY William H. Brock
THE HISTORY OF CHILDHOOD James Marten
THE HISTORY OF CINEMA Geoffrey Nowell-Smith
THE HISTORY OF LIFE Michael Benton
THE HISTORY OF MATHEMATICS Jacqueline Stedall
THE HISTORY OF MEDICINE William Bynum
THE HISTORY OF PHYSICS J. L. Heilbron
THE HISTORY OF TIME Leofranc Holford-Strevens
HIV AND AIDS Alan Whiteside
HOBBES Richard Tuck
HOLLYWOOD Peter Decherney
THE HOLY ROMAN EMPIRE Joachim Whaley
HOME Michael Allen Fox
HOMER Barbara Graziosi
HORMONES Martin Luck
HUMAN ANATOMY Leslie Klenerman
HUMAN EVOLUTION Bernard Wood
HUMAN RIGHTS Andrew Clapham
HUMANISM Stephen Law
HUME A. J. Ayer
HUMOUR Noël Carroll
THE ICE AGE Jamie Woodward
IDENTITY Florian Coulmas
IDEOLOGY Michael Freeden
THE IMMUNE SYSTEM Paul Klenerman
INDIAN CINEMA Ashish Rajadhyaksha
INDIAN PHILOSOPHY Sue Hamilton
THE INDUSTRIAL REVOLUTION Robert C. Allen
INFECTIOUS DISEASE Marta L. Wayne and Benjamin M. Bolker
INFINITY Ian Stewart
INFORMATION Luciano Floridi
INNOVATION Mark Dodgson and David Gann
INTELLECTUAL PROPERTY Siva Vaidhyanathan
INTELLIGENCE Ian J. Deary
INTERNATIONAL LAW Vaughan Lowe
INTERNATIONAL MIGRATION Khalid Koser
INTERNATIONAL RELATIONS Christian Reus-Smit
INTERNATIONAL SECURITY Christopher S. Browning
IRAN Ali M. Ansari
ISLAM Malise Ruthven
ISLAMIC HISTORY Adam Silverstein
ISLAMIC LAW Mashood A. Baderin
ISOTOPES Rob Ellam
ITALIAN LITERATURE Peter Hainsworth and David Robey
JESUS Richard Bauckham
JEWISH HISTORY David N. Myers
JOURNALISM Ian Hargreaves
JUDAISM Norman Solomon
JUNG Anthony Stevens
KABBALAH Joseph Dan
KAFKA Ritchie Robertson
KANT Roger Scruton
KEYNES Robert Skidelsky
KIERKEGAARD Patrick Gardiner
KNOWLEDGE Jennifer Nagel
THE KORAN Michael Cook
KOREA Michael J. Seth
LAKES Warwick F. Vincent

LANDSCAPE ARCHITECTURE
Ian H. Thompson
LANDSCAPES AND GEOMORPHOLOGY
Andrew Goudie and Heather Viles
LANGUAGES Stephen R. Anderson
LATE ANTIQUITY Gillian Clark
LAW Raymond Wacks
THE LAWS OF THERMODYNAMICS
Peter Atkins
LEADERSHIP Keith Grint
LEARNING Mark Haselgrove
LEIBNIZ Maria Rosa Antognazza
LEO TOLSTOY Liza Knapp
LIBERALISM Michael Freeden
LIGHT Ian Walmsley
LINCOLN Allen C. Guelzo
LINGUISTICS Peter Matthews
LITERARY THEORY Jonathan Culler
LOCKE John Dunn
LOGIC Graham Priest
LOVE Ronald de Sousa
MACHIAVELLI Quentin Skinner
MADNESS Andrew Scull
MAGIC Owen Davies
MAGNA CARTA Nicholas Vincent
MAGNETISM Stephen Blundell
MALTHUS Donald Winch
MAMMALS T. S. Kemp
MANAGEMENT John Hendry
MAO Delia Davin
MARINE BIOLOGY Philip V. Mladenov
MARKETING
Kenneth Le Meunier-FitzHugh
THE MARQUIS DE SADE John Phillips
MARTIN LUTHER Scott H. Hendrix
MARTYRDOM Jolyon Mitchell
MARX Peter Singer
MATERIALS Christopher Hall
MATHEMATICAL FINANCE
Mark H. A. Davis
MATHEMATICS Timothy Gowers
MATTER Geoff Cottrell
THE MAYA Matthew Restall and Amara Solari
THE MEANING OF LIFE
Terry Eagleton
MEASUREMENT David Hand
MEDICAL ETHICS Michael Dunn and Tony Hope
MEDICAL LAW Charles Foster
MEDIEVAL BRITAIN John Gillingham and Ralph A. Griffiths
MEDIEVAL LITERATURE
Elaine Treharne
MEDIEVAL PHILOSOPHY
John Marenbon
MEMORY Jonathan K. Foster
METAPHYSICS Stephen Mumford
METHODISM William J. Abraham
THE MEXICAN REVOLUTION
Alan Knight
MICHAEL FARADAY
Frank A. J. L. James
MICROBIOLOGY Nicholas P. Money
MICROECONOMICS Avinash Dixit
MICROSCOPY Terence Allen
THE MIDDLE AGES Miri Rubin
MILITARY JUSTICE Eugene R. Fidell
MILITARY STRATEGY
Antulio J. Echevarria II
MINERALS David Vaughan
MIRACLES Yujin Nagasawa
MODERN ARCHITECTURE
Adam Sharr
MODERN ART David Cottington
MODERN BRAZIL Anthony W. Pereira
MODERN CHINA Rana Mitter
MODERN DRAMA
Kirsten E. Shepherd-Barr
MODERN FRANCE
Vanessa R. Schwartz
MODERN INDIA Craig Jeffrey
MODERN IRELAND Senia Pašeta
MODERN ITALY Anna Cento Bull
MODERN JAPAN
Christopher Goto-Jones
MODERN LATIN AMERICAN LITERATURE
Roberto González Echevarría
MODERN WAR Richard English
MODERNISM Christopher Butler
MOLECULAR BIOLOGY
Aysha Divan and Janice A. Royds
MOLECULES Philip Ball
MONASTICISM Stephen J. Davis
THE MONGOLS Morris Rossabi
MONTAIGNE William M. Hamlin
MOONS David A. Rothery
MORMONISM
Richard Lyman Bushman
MOUNTAINS Martin F. Price

MUHAMMAD Jonathan A. C. Brown
MULTICULTURALISM Ali Rattansi
MULTILINGUALISM John C. Maher
MUSIC Nicholas Cook
MYTH Robert A. Segal
NAPOLEON David Bell
THE NAPOLEONIC WARS Mike Rapport
NATIONALISM Steven Grosby
NATIVE AMERICAN LITERATURE Sean Teuton
NAVIGATION Jim Bennett
NAZI GERMANY Jane Caplan
NELSON MANDELA Elleke Boehmer
NEOLIBERALISM Manfred B. Steger and Ravi K. Roy
NETWORKS Guido Caldarelli and Michele Catanzaro
THE NEW TESTAMENT Luke Timothy Johnson
THE NEW TESTAMENT AS LITERATURE Kyle Keefer
NEWTON Robert Iliffe
NIELS BOHR J. L. Heilbron
NIETZSCHE Michael Tanner
NINETEENTH-CENTURY BRITAIN Christopher Harvie and H. C. G. Matthew
THE NORMAN CONQUEST George Garnett
NORTH AMERICAN INDIANS Theda Perdue and Michael D. Green
NORTHERN IRELAND Marc Mulholland
NOTHING Frank Close
NUCLEAR PHYSICS Frank Close
NUCLEAR POWER Maxwell Irvine
NUCLEAR WEAPONS Joseph M. Siracusa
NUMBER THEORY Robin Wilson
NUMBERS Peter M. Higgins
NUTRITION David A. Bender
OBJECTIVITY Stephen Gaukroger
OCEANS Dorrik Stow
THE OLD TESTAMENT Michael D. Coogan
THE ORCHESTRA D. Kern Holoman
ORGANIC CHEMISTRY Graham Patrick
ORGANIZATIONS Mary Jo Hatch
ORGANIZED CRIME Georgios A. Antonopoulos and Georgios Papanicolaou
ORTHODOX CHRISTIANITY A. Edward Siecienski
OVID Llewelyn Morgan
PAGANISM Owen Davies
PAIN Rob Boddice
THE PALESTINIAN-ISRAELI CONFLICT Martin Bunton
PANDEMICS Christian W. McMillen
PARTICLE PHYSICS Frank Close
PAUL E. P. Sanders
PEACE Oliver P. Richmond
PENTECOSTALISM William K. Kay
PERCEPTION Brian Rogers
THE PERIODIC TABLE Eric R. Scerri
PHILOSOPHICAL METHOD Timothy Williamson
PHILOSOPHY Edward Craig
PHILOSOPHY IN THE ISLAMIC WORLD Peter Adamson
PHILOSOPHY OF BIOLOGY Samir Okasha
PHILOSOPHY OF LAW Raymond Wacks
PHILOSOPHY OF PHYSICS David Wallace
PHILOSOPHY OF SCIENCE Samir Okasha
PHILOSOPHY OF RELIGION Tim Bayne
PHOTOGRAPHY Steve Edwards
PHYSICAL CHEMISTRY Peter Atkins
PHYSICS Sidney Perkowitz
PILGRIMAGE Ian Reader
PLAGUE Paul Slack
PLANETS David A. Rothery
PLANTS Timothy Walker
PLATE TECTONICS Peter Molnar
PLATO Julia Annas
POETRY Bernard O'Donoghue
POLITICAL PHILOSOPHY David Miller
POLITICS Kenneth Minogue
POPULISM Cas Mudde and Cristóbal Rovira Kaltwasser
POSTCOLONIALISM Robert Young
POSTMODERNISM Christopher Butler

POSTSTRUCTURALISM Catherine Belsey
POVERTY Philip N. Jefferson
PREHISTORY Chris Gosden
PRESOCRATIC PHILOSOPHY Catherine Osborne
PRIVACY Raymond Wacks
PROBABILITY John Haigh
PROGRESSIVISM Walter Nugent
PROHIBITION W. J. Rorabaugh
PROJECTS Andrew Davies
PROTESTANTISM Mark A. Noll
PSYCHIATRY Tom Burns
PSYCHOANALYSIS Daniel Pick
PSYCHOLOGY Gillian Butler and Freda McManus
PSYCHOLOGY OF MUSIC Elizabeth Hellmuth Margulis
PSYCHOPATHY Essi Viding
PSYCHOTHERAPY Tom Burns and Eva Burns-Lundgren
PUBLIC ADMINISTRATION Stella Z. Theodoulou and Ravi K. Roy
PUBLIC HEALTH Virginia Berridge
PURITANISM Francis J. Bremer
THE QUAKERS Pink Dandelion
QUANTUM THEORY John Polkinghorne
RACISM Ali Rattansi
RADIOACTIVITY Claudio Tuniz
RASTAFARI Ennis B. Edmonds
READING Belinda Jack
THE REAGAN REVOLUTION Gil Troy
REALITY Jan Westerhoff
RECONSTRUCTION Allen C. Guelzo
THE REFORMATION Peter Marshall
REFUGEES Gil Loescher
RELATIVITY Russell Stannard
RELIGION Thomas A. Tweed
RELIGION IN AMERICA Timothy Beal
THE RENAISSANCE Jerry Brotton
RENAISSANCE ART Geraldine A. Johnson
RENEWABLE ENERGY Nick Jelley
REPTILES T.S. Kemp
REVOLUTIONS Jack A. Goldstone
RHETORIC Richard Toye
RISK Baruch Fischhoff and John Kadvany
RITUAL Barry Stephenson
RIVERS Nick Middleton
ROBOTICS Alan Winfield
ROCKS Jan Zalasiewicz
ROMAN BRITAIN Peter Salway
THE ROMAN EMPIRE Christopher Kelly
THE ROMAN REPUBLIC David M. Gwynn
ROMANTICISM Michael Ferber
ROUSSEAU Robert Wokler
RUSSELL A. C. Grayling
THE RUSSIAN ECONOMY Richard Connolly
RUSSIAN HISTORY Geoffrey Hosking
RUSSIAN LITERATURE Catriona Kelly
THE RUSSIAN REVOLUTION S. A. Smith
THE SAINTS Simon Yarrow
SAMURAI Michael Wert
SAVANNAS Peter A. Furley
SCEPTICISM Duncan Pritchard
SCHIZOPHRENIA Chris Frith and Eve Johnstone
SCHOPENHAUER Christopher Janaway
SCIENCE AND RELIGION Thomas Dixon
SCIENCE FICTION David Seed
THE SCIENTIFIC REVOLUTION Lawrence M. Principe
SCOTLAND Rab Houston
SECULARISM Andrew Copson
SEXUAL SELECTION Marlene Zuk and Leigh W. Simmons
SEXUALITY Véronique Mottier
SHAKESPEARE'S COMEDIES Bart van Es
SHAKESPEARE'S SONNETS AND POEMS Jonathan F. S. Post
SHAKESPEARE'S TRAGEDIES Stanley Wells
SIKHISM Eleanor Nesbitt
SILENT FILM Donna Kornhaber
THE SILK ROAD James A. Millward
SLANG Jonathon Green
SLEEP Steven W. Lockley and Russell G. Foster
SMELL Matthew Cobb
SOCIAL AND CULTURAL ANTHROPOLOGY John Monaghan and Peter Just

SOCIAL PSYCHOLOGY Richard J. Crisp
SOCIAL WORK Sally Holland and Jonathan Scourfield
SOCIALISM Michael Newman
SOCIOLINGUISTICS John Edwards
SOCIOLOGY Steve Bruce
SOCRATES C. C. W. Taylor
SOFT MATTER Tom McLeish
SOUND Mike Goldsmith
SOUTHEAST ASIA James R. Rush
THE SOVIET UNION Stephen Lovell
THE SPANISH CIVIL WAR Helen Graham
SPANISH LITERATURE Jo Labanyi
SPINOZA Roger Scruton
SPIRITUALITY Philip Sheldrake
SPORT Mike Cronin
STARS Andrew King
STATISTICS David J. Hand
STEM CELLS Jonathan Slack
STOICISM Brad Inwood
STRUCTURAL ENGINEERING David Blockley
STUART BRITAIN John Morrill
THE SUN Philip Judge
SUPERCONDUCTIVITY Stephen Blundell
SUPERSTITION Stuart Vyse
SYMMETRY Ian Stewart
SYNAESTHESIA Julia Simner
SYNTHETIC BIOLOGY Jamie A. Davies
SYSTEMS BIOLOGY Eberhard O. Voit
TAXATION Stephen Smith
TEETH Peter S. Ungar
TELESCOPES Geoff Cottrell
TERRORISM Charles Townshend
THEATRE Marvin Carlson
THEOLOGY David F. Ford
THINKING AND REASONING Jonathan St B. T. Evans
THOMAS AQUINAS Fergus Kerr
THOUGHT Tim Bayne
TIBETAN BUDDHISM Matthew T. Kapstein
TIDES David George Bowers and Emyr Martyn Roberts
TOCQUEVILLE Harvey C. Mansfield
TOPOLOGY Richard Earl
TRAGEDY Adrian Poole
TRANSLATION Matthew Reynolds
THE TREATY OF VERSAILLES Michael S. Neiberg
TRIGONOMETRY Glen Van Brummelen
THE TROJAN WAR Eric H. Cline
TRUST Katherine Hawley
THE TUDORS John Guy
TWENTIETH-CENTURY BRITAIN Kenneth O. Morgan
TYPOGRAPHY Paul Luna
THE UNITED NATIONS Jussi M. Hanhimäki
UNIVERSITIES AND COLLEGES David Palfreyman and Paul Temple
THE U.S. CIVIL WAR Louis P. Masur
THE U.S. CONGRESS Donald A. Ritchie
THE U.S. CONSTITUTION David J. Bodenhamer
THE U.S. SUPREME COURT Linda Greenhouse
UTILITARIANISM Katarzyna de Lazari-Radek and Peter Singer
UTOPIANISM Lyman Tower Sargent
VETERINARY SCIENCE James Yeates
THE VIKINGS Julian D. Richards
THE VIRTUES Craig A. Boyd and Kevin Timpe
VIRUSES Dorothy H. Crawford
VOLCANOES Michael J. Branney and Jan Zalasiewicz
VOLTAIRE Nicholas Cronk
WAR AND RELIGION Jolyon Mitchell and Joshua Rey
WAR AND TECHNOLOGY Alex Roland
WATER John Finney
WAVES Mike Goldsmith
WEATHER Storm Dunlop
THE WELFARE STATE David Garland
WILLIAM SHAKESPEARE Stanley Wells
WITCHCRAFT Malcolm Gaskill
WITTGENSTEIN A. C. Grayling
WORK Stephen Fineman
WORLD MUSIC Philip Bohlman
THE WORLD TRADE ORGANIZATION Amrita Narlikar
WORLD WAR II Gerhard L. Weinberg
WRITING AND SCRIPT Andrew Robinson
ZIONISM Michael Stanislawski

Available soon:

HUMAN PHYSIOLOGY Jamie A. Davies
THE ARCTIC Klaus Dodds and Jamie Woodwood
HORROR Darryl Jones
DIPLOMATIC HISTORY Joseph M. Siracusa
BLASPHEMY Yvonne Sherwood

For more information visit our website

www.oup.com/vsi/

Michael Wert

SAMURAI

A Very Short Introduction

OXFORD
UNIVERSITY PRESS

OXFORD
UNIVERSITY PRESS

Oxford University Press is a department of the University of Oxford. It furthers the University's objective of excellence in research, scholarship, and education by publishing worldwide. Oxford is a registered trade mark of Oxford University Press in the UK and certain other countries.

Published in the United States of America by Oxford University Press 198 Madison Avenue, New York, NY 10016, United States of America.

This book was published in hardcover as *Samurai: A Concise History* (2019).

Library of Congress Cataloging-in-Publication Data

Names: Wert, Michael, author.
Title: Samurai : a very short introduction / Michael Wert.
Description: New York, NY : Oxford University Press, [2021] | Series: Very short introductions | Includes bibliographical references and index.
Identifiers: LCCN 2020048484 (print) | LCCN 2020048485 (ebook) | ISBN 9780190685072 (paperback) | ISBN 9780190685089 (ebook) | ISBN 9780190685096 (epub)
Subjects: LCSH: Samurai. | Japan—History, Military.
Classification: LCC DS827.S3 W478 2021 (print) | LCC DS827.S3 (ebook) | DDC 952/.025—dc23
LC record available at https://lccn.loc.gov/2020048484
LC ebook record available at https://lccn.loc.gov/2020048485

1 3 5 7 9 8 6 4 2

Printed in Great Britain by Ashford Colour Press Ltd., Gosport, Hants., on acid-free paper

To my wife, Yuko Kojima Wert

Contents

List of Illustrations

Introduction

In the climactic battle scene at the end of the movie *The Last Samurai* (2003), the protagonist, a samurai rebel, leads his army of warriors as they charge to certain death against the newly formed, modern government army. Wearing only their traditional clothing and armed with bows, swords, and spears, they are mowed down by Gatling guns and howitzers as the government's general, himself an ex-samurai, looks on anxiously. This scene has all the familiar tropes in the global fantasy about samurai: tradition versus modernity, hand-to-hand fighting versus guns, and a celebration of honorable death. The event depicted in the film is a historical one, the War of the Southwest in Japan in 1877, when ex-samurai refused to follow a series of laws that stripped all samurai of their privileged status and accompanying symbols; no more wearing swords in public or maintaining topknot hairstyles. A more accurate description of the battle scene flips the cinematic one—the modernized government army took shelter in a castle, the most traditional of defenses, while ex-samurai rebels bombarded them with cannon from outside. As with anything else, the historical depiction is more interesting than the popularized one.

Samurai seem ubiquitous in popular culture; from the novel and television show *Shogun* (1980) to *The Last Samurai* and the successful PlayStation 4 game *Ghost of Tsushima* (2020), audiences never seem to tire of them. They even appear in the most unlikely places; the corporate name of a local coffee shop chain in Milwaukee, Wisconsin, is Giri, which the founder claims "comes from the Samurai code of honor, Bushido, and can be translated to mean 'social obligation.'" It sounds nice, but "obligation" was simply a way to convince samurai to obey their lords no matter the danger or, more likely, the drudgery.

There is no shortage of websites on samurai, and one can hardly throw a rock without hitting some martial art instructor with a distinctive view on the samurai. There are plenty of glossy books that give an overview of some aspect of samurai battles, warfare, castles, and the like, but sifting through what is reliable and what is not can be a chore. On the other hand, scholarly books tend to require too much background information, familiarity with not only Japanese but also Chinese history, religion, and art, disciplinary jargon, and, for some older history books, significant language commitment.

I will describe how samurai changed from, roughly, the eighth to the mid-nineteenth centuries, impart a sense of warrior diversity, and dispel common myths, such as the so-called bushido samurai code, swords as the "soul of the samurai," and supposed fighting prowess. Not all periods of warrior history are covered equally; there are more details of samurai life from the seventeenth through nineteenth centuries (the early modern period) because most depictions of samurai in the West coincide with warriors from that period, and scholars know more about early modern Japan than about the medieval period (ninth through fifteenth centuries). There are so many documents from the eighteenth and nineteenth centuries that one can buy them on internet auction sites for tens of dollars. A recent auction for a collection of hundreds of documents from the eighteenth and nineteenth centuries, belonging to a single family, sold on Yahoo Auction for 73,000 yen, about $660. Some texts from early modern Japan even end up in the trash. After the earthquake, tsunami, and

Fukushima nuclear disaster on March 11, 2011, local historians scrambled to photograph historical documents found in dilapidated storehouses slated for destruction and rebuilding. There were so many documents that local museums and universities did not have room to keep those deemed unimportant, and hence they risked being thrown out. Documents from before the seventeenth century are occasionally discovered but in ever fewer numbers, and they are treated with greater care.

A final word about conventions. In Japanese, the surname precedes the given name. I use the term *warrior* for the ninth through sixteenth centuries and *samurai* for the seventeenth through nineteenth centuries, when they existed as a narrowly defined social status group. *Warlord* and *lord* both refer to *daimyo*, military leaders who held territory and engaged in warfare during the fifteenth and sixteenth centuries, but by the early seventeenth century, they had become decidedly unwarlike governors. In other words, I split warrior history into two imperfect halves, the medieval and early modern periods, with the early seventeenth century as the dividing line. That is when the category of warrior narrowed, fundamentally changing for this group their culture and relationship to the rest of the Japanese population.

Chapter 1
Becoming those who served

Colloquially, even in Japan, the term *samurai* is used as a synonym for "warrior," but this is incorrect. *Samurai* originally had a very narrow meaning, referring to anyone who served a noble, even in a nonmilitary capacity. Gradually it became a title for military servants of warrior families—in fact, a warrior of elite stature in pre-seventeenth-century Japan would have been insulted to be called a "samurai." There were other more common terms for warriors in classical and medieval Japan that reflected their various duties to the state, nobility, and other superiors. Most specialists in Japan and in the West use the generic term *bushi*, which means "warrior."

Warrior is a usefully ambiguous term for referring to a broad group of people, before the seventeenth century, with some military function. This includes anyone expected to provide military service to the state when needed and who received official recognition from a ruling authority to do so, such as the nobility and court in Kyoto or religious institutions. Even the term *warrior* is imprecise because it incorrectly suggests that warfare was this group's sole occupation. Depending on the time period and status, warriors alternatively governed, traded, farmed, painted, wrote, tutored, and engaged in shady activities.

Another caution when using the term *warrior* is the moral value that modern people attach to the concept. The US military uses "warrior" in its various training programs, such as "Warrior Mind Training," a meditation program created for soldiers to help them cope with posttraumatic stress disorder and to prepare them for the rigors of combat. The developer used the image of the samurai to sell the program, "rooting it in the ancient Samurai code of self-discipline." No such code existed. Even phrases used ironically assume the existence of an authentic admirable warrior image—for example, "weekend warrior," suggesting that one is a normal boring person during the week but becomes some other, more primal person on the weekend. In this usage, a warrior is something one *is*, not an occupation one *does*.

But throughout Japanese history, people often despised warriors. Artists and writers portrayed warriors as beasts, no better than dogs, uncouth and murderous. Warriors pillaged, looted, and sometimes murdered their way through villages. They found no love among peasants, who feared warriors because peasants suffered the most from their looting, pillaging, and collateral damage. Ironically, it was only during an age of relative peace, in early modern Japan (1600–1868), that common people began to admire and imitate samurai.

Of course, warriors fought in combat, but in reality they spent most of their time doing something else. That could mean trying to improve their family's position in an elite society dominated by nobility, managing farmers on their estates, or, for the lowliest warriors, even engaging in occasional grift. The limit of samurai activities was determined by the definition of "warrior" as it changed over time. A samurai traveling back in time from the nineteenth century to the ninth might hardly be recognized as belonging to the same category of people.

Warriors of the distant past became a source of entertainment, anxiety, and inspiration for samurai living in later times. One samurai commentator in the early eighteenth century, an era of peace, complained of his contemporaries, "So many men now seem to have the pulse of a woman," nothing like the real warrior men of the previous century, a time of war. In the thirteenth century, a Buddhist nun, Hōjō Masako, invoked the legacy of her late husband Minamoto Yoritomo as a warrior founding father of sorts who fought against a threat from an emperor in Kyoto. And let's not forget the material appeal of the past; samurai of higher status delighted in purchasing a sword or tea bowl once owned by famous warriors.

Warriors used military skills as a means of advancing their careers. Politically, they were outsiders, used as tools by powerful nobles who needed them as muscle to police their lands or to act as a check on other noble families intent on taking land by force. Much of Japan technically belonged to the emperor (*tennō*, literally "heavenly sovereign"), who, according to ancient mythology, was descended from gods, and warriors protected the interests of the emperor's regime based in the ancient capital cities of Nara, Nagaoka, and from 794, Kyoto. They guarded against outbreaks of violence close to the capital, attacked anyone in the provinces far from Kyoto who might threaten the regime, and campaigned against the many "barbaric" tribes located on the outskirts of Japan in the northeast or southwest.

The term *warrior* typically does not include others who lived by violence—namely, mercenaries, bandits, and pirates. But before the seventeenth century, a person's status was not so neatly defined. Some people temporarily connected to a ruling institution could legally participate in warfare, governance, and commerce. For example, though most warrior and royal authorities depicted pirates as violent bandits operating at sea, they sometimes engaged in warfare on behalf of a warrior regime called a shogunate, a religious institution such as a Buddhist temple, or a noble ensconced in the capital, Kyoto. They monopolized sea-based trade, established rules of conduct and expectations from people living along waterways, and wielded authority like a warlord or warrior bureaucracy.

A debate about warrior origins has raged in both the Japanese and English language scholarship on premodern Japan due, in part, to how one defines *samurai*. Were they simply a carryover from ancient soldiers? The earliest evidence for warrior-soldiers predates written history and Japan itself. Terracotta figures (*haniwa*) depicting soldiers, servants, and animals were placed outside tombs that dotted the ancient burial landscape between the third and sixth centuries. The soldiers' arms and armor reflect the influence of contemporary warriors in China and the Korean kingdoms and share a common style that shows the existence of some primitive regime that influenced mostly central and southwest Japan. Hunters and landholders from the eastern provinces? Or professional warriors hired by the Kyoto court? For the sake of argument, it is safe to say that private military specialists emerged as a permanent feature in Japanese history around the ninth century when some of them began wielding authority over others rather than serving as mere soldiers.

Written evidence for warrior history can be traced to the late eighth and early ninth centuries, when the early Japanese state adopted the administrative structure of Tang dynasty China (618–907), the dominant cultural and political power in East Asia. In addition to adapting the various court titles, noble ranks, bureaucratic structures, and culture, the early Japanese sovereigns copied Tang military organization. The court required men to serve in provincial units in times of need. Though a conscript army existed on paper, most showed up only for occasional short-term assignments of up to thirty days or so—for example, to serve in the frontier guard. Most of the year they pursued their own livelihoods. Conscripts were supposed to supply their own weapons and equipment and did not spend much time training. Only officers worked in the military for long periods of time, and some historians have argued that those men were engaged in managerial work rather than intense military training or warfare. Much of the Tang administrative model was abandoned in Japan in the late eighth century and was gradually replaced over the next century and a half with specialist warriors.

In the broadest terms, several different types of warriors existed beginning in the early eighth century. Most warriors did not "own" land, per se, but received a portion of an estate's produce and the rights to collect—and skim—taxes from estates owned by absentee proprietors living in Kyoto. Some enjoyed relative freedom from interference by authorities in Kyoto or their representatives in the provinces. Some possessed land themselves and consigned some of that land to a non warrior noble family in Kyoto in exchange for patronage—that is, for guarantees that others would not stake a claim on a warrior's land. Still other warriors were themselves members of noble families, albeit of a lower rank than most of the powerful nobles who controlled the top bureaucratic positions in Kyoto. Of those, some had established local connections and alliances during a tenure as provincial governor and remained there permanently. They became warrior-lords and relied on minor warrior families while maintaining connections to allies and resources in Kyoto. As the center of rule and the largest city at the time, Kyoto wielded a centripetal force on elite clans throughout Japan. People with aristocratic Kyoto lineage occupied the top social strata in provincial society. Prominent families in the countryside worried about Kyoto-appointed governors sent to monitor them, and politics in Kyoto could threaten local access to wealth.

There was no single model for how these warriors organized themselves. Men might cooperate in bands of warriors connected by kinship, personal loyalty, or common enemies. Others worked together for noble families located in the capital city, provincial officials, or local strongmen. It is no surprise that the ability to fight and organize resources for a military campaign was more efficient among these specialized groups than among conscripts whose livelihoods were interrupted, not enhanced, by warfare. Eventually the state depended on these professionalized warrior groups for police and military functions. Dependency did not mean that warriors took authority away from the state, nor was it the beginning of the end for the royalty, as was once taught; the court and nobility were still in charge.

Most powerful warriors in classical and medieval Japan tended to be those who were themselves nobles and thus had little incentive to challenge the status quo of their community. Although they never achieved the upper echelons of noble ranking, many large, interconnected families that dominated Japan, such as the Taira and the Minamoto, were descended from sons of emperors cast aside because they were no longer in the running for the throne. An emperor bestowed a surname upon these sons who started clans of their own and followed careers common to noble families: serving as functionaries at court, working as important and influential Buddhist clergy, or becoming professional warriors. But not all families within a single surname, such as Minamoto, pursued the same career trajectory.

One might wonder, though, did any warrior try to overthrow the emperor in Kyoto or otherwise carve out a territory of his own, independent from the center? Taira Masakado was the first would-be rebel against the court. He lived in eastern Japan, not far from present-day Tokyo, surrounded by other Taira families who controlled land in the east. Some of them served as the imperial court's representatives. Masakado had once lived in Kyoto under the court's employment, but he was largely a man of the east, a land distant from the center of political and cultural power. What began as a conflict over land among different Taira families and Masakado's own relatives—fighting that the nobility in Kyoto largely ignored—turned into an act of rebellion in 935 when Masakado retaliated against Taira men who were the emperor's representatives. Masakado might not have intended to rebel against the emperor, nor did he have a force large enough to threaten Kyoto directly, but he declared himself the "new emperor" in the east, a career that did not last long—he was killed by a cousin in 940.

Another challenger to imperial and noble authority was Taira Kiyomori. He, too, was descended from an emperor and was raised in Kyoto like other aristocrats. When a succession dispute broke out within the imperial family over who would become the next emperor, Kiyomori led the forces of the victor; the losers, mostly under the control of Minamoto Yoshitomo, were sent into exiled or killed. What began as a clash against forces representing noble patrons turned into a rivalry between Kiyomori and Yoshitomo. Kiyomori beat Yoshitomo and began accumulating aristocratic titles, bureaucratic posts, and provincial landholdings. By the late 1170s, he had become a real threat to imperial power. In Kyoto, he placed allies in important positions not already under his direct control and tried, unsuccessfully, to move the capital to what is now Kobe. There he embarked on massive building projects, including his own headquarters and ports for trade with China. He was the first warrior-noble who attempted to dominate all warriors in Japan. He even put his own grandson, the child emperor Antoku, on the throne. The prince who had been passed up for succession when young Antoku was enthroned asked warriors to overthrow Kiyomori. That challenge started the so-called Gempei War (1180–85), which lasted longer, and was geographically broader, than any previous battle in Japanese history. It even outlasted Kiyomori, who died of natural causes in 1181.

No broadly conceived warrior identity existed before the Gempei War. At the top of warrior society, the most powerful families were themselves part of the aristocracy; the terms *warrior* and *nobility* were not mutually exclusive. For the most part, warriors with noble surnames such as Minamoto and Taira, who resided largely in the countryside, had no incentive to fight against the imperial institution that their ancestors had helped build. Many acted as bridges between Kyoto and the countryside; they feared relatives and neighbors and were hardly in a position to rise up against the imperial institution. At the other end of the social spectrum, the lowly nonaristocratic soldiers and mercenaries often engaged in nonmilitary work. Even midranking warriors shared little in common with their royal betters.

This situation changed to a degree after Minamoto Yoritomo emerged as the victor at the end of the Gempei War. He remained at his headquarters in Kamakura and is credited with creating the first warrior-centered regime, the Kamakura shogunate (1185–1333). Textbooks portray him as the originator of Japan's warrior identity, but that shared identity extended only to the warriors who gathered around him in Kamakura. This beginning of so-called warrior order was not orderly nor did it involve only warriors. But it represented a first step toward a broader notion of warrior culture and identity that would develop over the subsequent centuries.

Chapter 2
Early warrior authority

Minamoto Yoritomo's forces swept from eastern Japan to the west, defeating the Taira armies in 1185. With the help of Kyoto-born nobility and warrior allies, Yoritomo created a warrior regime that lasted until 1333, at which time several prominent warrior clans destroyed the Kamakura regime in the name of the emperor. The shogunate's leading men, first Yoritomo and then a series of regents ruling on behalf of weak titular leaders called shoguns, consolidated their control over Japan at the expense of the nobility. Thus, the typical story about Japan's first warrior regime centers on the institution of the shogunate and how it became the center of a putative "warrior order." It focuses on men who managed estates, created a primitive legal court, and interacted with noblemen as either employers, allies, or foes. In popular culture, these men tend to be in armor on a battlefield constantly engaged in combat. In reality, they spent less time fighting than movies and manga (Japanese graphic novels) would have us believe. The fullness of early warrior history is best captured through its women. All warrior households had military obligations, but those obligations were organized by family units in the broadest sense: large clans comprising women, retainers, and servants who fulfilled menial and complex duties. Military obligation included supplying food, clothing, and labor; it was not simply engaging in combat on the battlefield.

1. Tomoe Gozen is shown dressed in armor—depicted as a combatant rather than as a docile wife. The artist describes her "wielding her halberd like a water wheel."

Moreover, the survival of any warrior family depended on the efficient management of its wealth, smooth relations among allies, and, especially for elite warrior families, connections with nonwarrior aristocrats. Men dominated this process but could not do so without women. In one sense, women were used as objects, through marriage, to solidify an alliance between elite families. But a woman retained any possessions given to her during her marriage, and she continued to live on her parents' estate or in her own residence, often separately from her husband, making her far more independent than her samurai counterparts during later periods. Warrior wives also wielded tremendous influence on their family's position in society. For example, they acted on behalf of either dead or absent husbands; a widow could carry out her clan's military obligations.

Indeed, there might not have been a Kamakura shogunate without women. The Kyoto aristocratic custom of entrusting the future of one's child to female caretakers and their families provided Yoritomo with a stable of warrior and nonwarrior connections vital to his success. Since many of Yoritomo's male relatives were killed, he depended on the women who helped raise him as a child. They supplied him with wealth, male allies in his youth, and information from Kyoto. His mother was born into the Fujiwara clan, the most powerful noble family before the thirteenth century. Her status guaranteed Yoritomo's high position within the Minamoto clan because his father's other consorts were of lower noble blood. And when Kiyomori defeated the Minamoto clan, he spared Yoritomo, it is said, because Kiyomori's stepmother intervened on his behalf. Instead, he exiled Yoritomo to the Izu province in the east, far from Kyoto's center of wealth and power. There Yoritomo grew up under the watch of Hōjō Tokimasa, the twenty-two-year-old head of a minor, obscure family distantly related to the Taira. Like other Kyoto noblemen, Yoritomo was born into a pampered life and must have been shocked by his move to a very rural area as an adolescent.

Elite warrior families like the Minamoto followed the courtier model of marriage and child rearing in which women were at the center. In Kyoto noble culture, nannies and wet nurses came from minor noble families, and the boys placed in their care played and learned alongside these women's own children. Since the boys essentially grew up together, they often became trusted allies as adults despite differences in social status within the noble hierarchy. The noblewomen who knew Yoritomo as a child ensured that he would continue to maintain a decent life in Izu well into adulthood.

For example, one of Yoritomo's wet nurses, the nun Hiki, consistently sent him rice, a form of wealth. She controlled her family after her husband's death, and the heir that she adopted, Hiki Yoshikazu, became one of Yoritomo's closest allies and a top advisor in the shogunate after Yoritomo died. Likewise, her son-in-law, Adachi Morinaga, became a trusted advisor to Yoritomo, and his clan provided much-needed economic support to Yoritomo. Hiki's daughter even served as the wet nurse to Yoritomo's son, the second shogun Minamoto Yoriie. A third wet nurse mediated the connection between Yoritomo and her grandson, Miyoshi Yasunobu, who served Yoritomo in a bureaucratic rather than a military function. Indeed, the only older male relative Yoritomo could count on while in Izu was his maternal uncle, the Buddhist monk Yūhan, who sent a servant to Izu once a month to bring Yoritomo news from Kyoto.

Yoritomo was not destined for greatness even though warriors in later centuries would glorify him. He spent most of his adult life in obscurity. It was not until he reached his early thirties, fully middle-aged for the time period, that he attacked the Taira clan and began to create the Kamakura shogunate, an institution left incomplete during his lifetime. His background, supporters, and the political and economic environment for families in the east contributed to his success in elevating warrior authority, a process that continued long after his death.

Yoritomo gathered allies around him by taking advantage of their economic anxieties. Warrior families did not own land per se but could access land and its resources, human and material, through various managerial and policing duties granted to them by absentee landholders. Warriors did not control the appointment or transferring of those duties, nor could a warrior hope to rise into the upper echelons of nobility that would make him a proprietor. Taira Kiyomori, for example, could not be a landowner and merely appointed himself as protector and governor of lands. He had to imitate noble precedent by copying the Fujiwara family's practice of placing a grandson on the imperial throne.

Adding to economic insecurity were regional threats from neighboring rivals or family members who might take land or titles by force. It might seem counterintuitive, but the greatest threats came from within one's own clan. With no concept of primogeniture (the oldest son inheriting everything), the death of a clan leader might result in immediate infighting among cousins, uncles, and sons from different women who lived separately from their husbands. For lower-ranking warrior aristocrats or clans not based in and around Kyoto, sons were raised by the mother's family, and the wife's family vied for control over wealth and influence.

Thus, when an imperial prince, Mochihito, put out the call for people to oust Kiyomori from his position, those who responded took into consideration intra clan politics, connections to Kyoto nobility, and local rivalries when deciding if, and how, they would act. Yoritomo spent much of his time fighting relatives and clans traditionally allied to the Minamoto in the early stages of the Gempei War. From the beginning, other Minamoto men such as Yorimasa, who was defeated in 1180, and Yoritomo's cousin, Yoshinaka, also mobilized against Kiyomori, rivaling Yoritomo's efforts. Yoritomo gathered around him warriors whose loyalty he secured by promising them titles, access to land, and a pretext to attack local rivals. He provided an alternative to Kyoto-based authority for people living in the east. In fact, once the Taira troops captured and killed Prince Mochihito, the royal court, under Taira influence, declared Yoritomo a rebel. Thus, unlike Kiyomori, whose career was made within the bounds of the imperial government, Yoritomo could confiscate lands from his enemies instead of forfeiting them to the emperor.

The Gempei War did not unfold as one might expect. The initial protagonist, Mochihito, and antagonist, Kiyomori, died in 1180 and 1181, respectively. Mochihito and his Minamoto supporters were cornered and killed, while Kiyomori died of a fever so high, the literary version of the events in the *Tale of Heike* tells us that it was caused by the guardians and flames of hell coming to claim him.

Yoritomo was busy fighting local enemies and rivals, building a headquarters and bureaucracy in Kamakura until 1184, when he marched on Kyoto. In 1185, his half-brother Yoshitsune pursued the Taira as they retreated south from Kyoto. Yoshitsune, not Yoritomo, led the more spectacular battles, including the final one along the coast by the sea of Dan-no-Ura, far southwest from Kyoto and Kamakura. The Minamoto forces destroyed the remnants of the Taira clan, while the Taira noblewomen, one of them still holding onto the child emperor Antoku, Kiyomori's grandson, dived into the seas of Dan-no-Ura and drowned. So tragic was the defeat of Taira warriors, noblewomen, and servants that local legend claims the spirits of the Taira warriors imprinted themselves onto the carapace of small crabs.

The significance of the Gempei War in Japanese warrior history cannot be reduced to a neat list of losers and winners, or of gains and losses. The emperor had no choice but to recognize Yoritomo's emergence as Japan's dominant warrior, making him the "constable" (*shugo*) of all of Japan's provinces. He restored Yoritomo's court rank, eliminating his status as a rebel, and recognized his right to assign warriors as managers to estates

2. A popular legend tells how defeated Taira warriors turned into crabs like this one found in the seas around southwestern Japan. The crabs are said to contain the spirits of the angry, dead warriors, particularly those killed in the pivotal naval battle in the sea along Dan-no-Ura that ended the Gempei War (1180–85).

throughout Japan. But warriors did not control Japan; even Yoritomo coveted noble court rank and recognition from Kyoto. In his portrait he is dressed as an aristocrat, not as a warrior in battle dress. The war engendered a sense of unease for all elites, including Kyoto nobles, members of religious institutions, warriors, Yoritomo and his allies, and prominent local families. Rather than simply "serving" the Kyoto nobility, warriors now encroached on Kyoto's prerogatives of rule, a process that even Yoritomo could not control completely.

Yoritomo's Kamakura

Kamakura, a humble village with ancestral connections to the Minamoto, became a site of power during the 1180s. Called simply

"Ōkura Palace" at the time, it was the location of what is now referred to as the Kamakura shogunate, Japan's first warrior regime. Across Japan, warriors who wanted to benefit from Yoritomo's success declared that they too were his vassals, called "housemen" (*gokenin*), in an attempt to legitimize their local agendas. The shogunate's offices, staffed by minor nobles from Kyoto, monks, and warriors, managed applications for houseman status and tried to adjudicate lawsuits against warriors by other warriors and nonwarriors.

What makes the founding of the shogunate a watershed moment is that it forever changed how one group of warriors related to another. Although this change was limited to those who lived in the city of Kamakura itself, mostly Yoritomo's vassals and those who served the shogunate, it created opportunities for warriors to meet each other on a daily basis. Before the twelfth century, most warriors interacted only with family members, servants, and retainers who may have served them. Other than occasional guard duty in Kyoto or military campaigns, warriors of unrelated clans rarely encountered each other. In other words, the shogunate, especially Yoritomo's palace itself, became a place where warriors developed as a social group—an exclusive one. Most of these warriors were directly connected to Yoritomo. The palace functioned as a space for official meetings and social gatherings. It became a place to strengthen ties among warrior families, arrange marriages, and dole out punishment. The day-to-day business of running a government meshed with social events. For example, Yoritomo had one of his vassals murdered during a board game session (*sugoroku*). Outside the palace, warriors hunted together and engaged in ceremonies that had both pseudo-religious and martial functions—for example, bouts of sumo wrestling or shooting on horseback. These provided opportunities for warriors to strengthen the bonds to each other and to the shogunate, separate from the nonwarrior nobility in Kyoto. Nonetheless, connections to nobility in Kyoto, especially through marriage,

3. **Elite warriors in early Japan valued their court-appointed titles more than their status as warriors. The only way a viewer might guess that this is a portrait of a warrior, said to be Yoritomo, is from the short sword on his hip.**

remained important to warriors throughout the rest of Japanese history.

Not all of Yoritomo's vassals knew each other, and many falsely claimed to serve him. It was not until 1189, when he ordered his housemen to follow him into war against rebels in the northern city of Hiraizumi, that he could finally distinguish between those who were really housemen and those who were not. Housemen who refused his command were stripped of their titles and coveted privileges. For the most part, warriors were concerned about local issues and only secondarily about relations with the shogunate. Loyalty to the shogunate was sometimes loose and did not extend to the many warriors across Japan who were not Yoritomo's vassals.

Much like Kiyomori before him, Yoritomo placed nobles favorable to him in important bureaucratic posts in Kyoto while building his own independent headquarters. Yoritomo had no grand blueprint for his rule, and he demanded that warriors follow local practices and precedents established by the nobility. Moreover, Yoritomo's victory did not lead to an era of warrior dominance. He and the shogunate reined in warrior aspirations; they did not take over or destroy the Kyoto government. For the remainder of the twelfth century and part of the thirteenth, Kamakura was a junior ruling partner with Kyoto. Much of what defined Kamakura as a semibureaucratic regime developed after 1199, when Yoritomo died in a manner not unheard of among elite warriors—falling from a horse.

Hōjō's Kamakura

As was the custom for noble and elite warrior families alike, Yoritomo's sons were raised by women and the male relatives connected to their mother, the widowed nun Hōjō Masako. She was the closest personal connection between Yoritomo and the shogunate. This put her at the center of a struggle for control over the shogunate that included her brother (Yasutoki), her father (Tokimasa), her son (Yoriie) and his wife's family (the Hiki), and Yoritomo's allies. Although many vassals tried to uphold Yoritomo's legacy through Masako, others challenged that authority—blind loyalty was not the norm. Nearly a dozen people in the Hiki, Hōjō, and Minamoto families died in the succession disputes that followed, and Masako emerged as one of the few sources of continuity in shogunal politics from the late twelfth to the early thirteenth centuries.

Masako, far from being a protective mother supporting her son Yoriie, the second shogun, was closer to her birth family, the Hōjō. According to the late thirteenth-century historical chronicle *Mirror of the East*, Yoriie was an ineffectual leader. Not long after his father's death, Yoriie sent a close vassal of Yoritomo on a false errand in the hope of taking the man's lover while he was gone. The vassal returned to Kamakura having learned about the ruse, and Yoriie planned to preemptively attack the vassal's mansion. Masako occupied the vassal's residence to stop her son's attack and then berated Yoriie in writing. She also made the vassal promise that he would not retaliate at some later date. Even Minamoto men, such as Yoritomo's half-brother Zenjo, sought Masako's protection. She considered Zenjo a potential threat to her family, however, and rejected him; he was eventually hunted down and killed.

Masako's efforts on behalf of her brother, rather than her son Yoriie, pushed Yoriie closer to his in-laws, the Hiki, thus setting the scene for a showdown between the Hiki and Hōjō. The Hiki used him to obtain posts in the shogunate and hold sway over his sons who would inherit the shogun title. For example, the Hiki patriarch, Yoshikazu, envisioned his grandson inheriting the shogun title after Yoriie, thus putting the Hiki in a dominant position in the shogunate. But Hōjō Tokimasa had the same idea, and under his orders, Yoriie's heir was executed, as were some Hiki family members. In 1203, Masako and her father Tokimasa forced Yoriie to retire after he fell ill. And when Tokimasa heard that Yoriie was planning to have him assassinated, Yoriie too was killed, leaving the Hōjō victorious. Naturally, Tokimasa, as the Hōjō patriarch, had his own ideas about the shogunate's future: he wanted children from his second wife to control it. But Masako preferred her brother. In 1205 she had her father arrested and she controlled the shogunate alongside her brother Yoshitoki.

Tension among warrior families was complicated by warrior connections to the Kyoto establishment. Once Yoriie fell ill and died, the last remaining son of Yoritomo was anointed shogun, the eleven-year-old Sanetomo. But he was less a warrior than an aristocrat, engaging in activities typically associated with Kyoto nobility. He studied classical poetry assiduously, learning from one of the greatest classical poets, Fujiwara no Teika. And he maintained relatively close ties to Kyoto nobles including the emperor Go-Toba. Similar to his father, Sanetomo held the title "shogun" in less esteem than positions awarded to him within the noble hierarchy. He even surpassed Yoritomo in that realm, having received a prestigious administrative title, "Minister of the Right," a position, largely ceremonial at this time, that oversaw Kyoto's Council of State. He did not enjoy that title for even a few hours, however; his nephew, Yoriie's son, murdered him during the ceremony, blaming his uncle for his father's death. Thus Yoritomo's line ended with Sanetomo's murder in 1219.

Sanetomo's relationship to the nobility represented a potential high point between the court and the shogunate. Since he did not produce an heir, Masako brokered an agreement with Go-Toba in 1218 that would have resulted in an imperial prince becoming the fourth shogun. This would have been an attractive possibility to Go-Toba, who could then influence both a new emperor and a new shogun. Instead, Sanetomo's murder became an opportunity for Go-Toba to accomplish what Go-Shirakawa had tried to do in the aftermath of the Gempei War—bring warriors to heel under Kyoto authority.

The Jōkyū order

Go-Toba's attack against the shogunate, known as the Jōkyū War (1221), named after the reign year, is hardly worth mentioning as a military event. It pitted Go-Toba's hodgepodge of warriors, some Kamakura housemen, and many warriors from the west unaffiliated with the shogunate against the Hōjō and their supporters. Each army had about a thousand soldiers and the fighting lasted less than a month. But it was significant for its role in shifting power away from the emperor and court in favor of the shogunate. The crown prince, an emperor, and three retired emperors were all banished. Here again, Masako seems to have played a decisive role, if the stories of her speech are to be believed, by appealing to the Hōjō fighters' sense of loyalty to her late husband. Loyalty might have motivated some warriors on both sides, but others used the war as a pretext to attack rivals. Moreover, a Go-Toba victory would probably have curtailed warrior authority throughout Japan, not enhanced it. At any rate, it took the Hōjō army only a month to defeat Go-Toba's forces.

Many of the titles, positions, and bureaucratic structures of the Kamakura shogunate were fully developed during the thirteenth century under the Hōjō after their victory. The Hōjō did not conduct themselves with impunity, yet warrior families were eager to maintain stability in the countryside and protect themselves. Even if they did not wholeheartedly support the Hōjō, they were at least willing to cooperate with the shogunate for the time being. The shogunate responded to these anxieties by incorporating a broader range of warriors into the shogunate's rule.

The Hōjō placed more warrior-managers, including at least one woman, on estates throughout Japan, particularly among those of Go-Toba's defeated supporters and in regions where there had been none before the shogunate was established. Rather than follow the myriad pre-Jōkyū customs for tax collection, the shogunate attempted to standardize collection across all estates.

These expansive policies could not have worked under the early shogunate, when Yoritomo and his immediate successors had neither the manpower nor the know-how to challenge Kyoto precedent. In those days, the shogunate followed Kyoto's lead, ruling with Kyoto rather than against it. After the Jōkyū war, however, the shogunate expanded warrior authority and intensified its penetration throughout Japan.

The Hōjō empowered military governors to stop rebellions, to hunt down criminals, to defend the coasts against pirates, and, in distant southern Japan, to try and judge criminals. These military governors could move across estate borders and public land, which local warriors could not do. Nonetheless, appointments to the military governor position were not permanent; governors did not have the power to tax and could not act independently of the shogunate or infringe upon nonwarrior lands.

For example, the Kamakura shogunate's first legal code, the *Laws and Regulations for Judgment* (*Goseibai Shikimoku*), was not enacted until 1232, as a response to the Jōkyū War. Although it is typically described as a set of military laws, it reflects many issues that had been common in the Kyoto bureaucracy. Calling it a *law* overestimates the extent of its impact over the diverse groups of people called *warriors*. The term *law* did not carry with it the meanings it does in the modern world; for example, there were few mechanisms for enforcing rules in the premodern world nor was there a legal culture saturating daily life as there is today. No premodern government could enforce, or even conceive of, the monitoring and categorization of human life and property, from birth to death, as a modern government does. Mostly, the *Laws and Regulations for Judgment* established expectations and consequences laid out for military governors and land stewards—upper and middle management. Many warriors in places far from Kamakura simply ignored the code. Nonetheless, the *Laws and Regulations* marked the first time that a warrior regime in Japan created a model for behavior applicable to warriors across space and time; warrior leaders and intellectuals studied it up to the nineteenth century, long after the Kamakura shogunate had collapsed.

As a *legal* document, in keeping with the practice by the shogunate since its beginning, it emphasized following precedent. "Governors of provinces and estate [nonwarrior] proprietors may exercise their normal jurisdiction without referring to the shogunate authorities." In fact, such proprietors were told that the shogunate would not even entertain requests from temples or shrines that wanted guidance from the shogunate.

The code attempted to restrain newly empowered housemen and administrators after the Jōkyū War. Stewards found skimming tax collections or collecting more tax than was required "shall be deprived of their posts." Even if their deputies committed crimes or otherwise "contravene[d] the laws and precedents," the steward would be held responsible if he knew about it and tried to shield the deputy. Military governors who confiscated property for some offense without making a proper report would "be dealt with criminally."

In the mid-fourteenth century, a trial handbook titled *A Book for Those Unskilled in Legal Matters* (*Sata Mirensho*) was created that defined simple terms like *plaintiff* and more complicated concepts such as miscellaneous civil cases and criminal cases. Among the civil cases were "money or grain loans with interest; sale of paddy fields, slaves, or semi-free workers; and abduction of servants"; the criminal cases included "rebellion, night attacks, robbery with violence, secret theft, brigandry, piracy, murder, arson, battery, wounding with a sharp weapon, arson, seizing and raping women, creating a panic and stealing people's valuables as they flee, or harvesting another's paddy or dry field."

And what was life like for warriors across Japan? It depended on whom you worked for and your position within that local hierarchy. The shogunate expected its housemen to spend several months during the year performing guard duty in Kyoto, providing service to a provincial governor or perhaps working on an estate in some bureaucratic and police function. Men might be rotated through different positions in order to learn the full range of duties required of shogunal vassals. Warriors who were not directly connected to the shogunate worked in similar capacities locally, serving various functions for a noble family, a Buddhist temple complex, or powerful clans in the countryside with loose or nonexistent ties to Kyoto nobility or the Kamakura shogunate. Some warriors worked directly for the emperor. Since Japan was not in a constant state of war, however, duties tended to be mundane or physical; many warriors worked in agriculture alongside commoners.

Most warriors struggled economically. Estate stewards were typically paid from the taxes they collected, and they often abused their tax collecting power. Economically, clans that had access to land suffered after several generations as the custom of equal inheritance among sons and daughters had whittled away the family estate. Building projects, patronizing Buddhist temples, buying artwork from China, participating in courtly rituals: these were just some of the drains on elite warrior wealth that forced them to borrow money from local merchants, an indebtedness that was never resolved. Nor could their traditional sources of income—namely, produce from land—maintain pace with a growing commercial economy. These problems did not occur suddenly, but they were exacerbated by the Mongol invasions.

The Mongol incursion

In 1215, Kublai Khan, the grandson of Chinggis Khan and leader of the Mongols, achieved what his grandfather could not: the conquest of China. From Beijing, Kublai embarked on several decades of invasions with mixed success. He subjugated Korea, for example, but despite repeated attempts, failed to conquer Java, the Vietnamese kingdoms of Dai Viet and Champa, and Japan. Warrior history was never completely separate from events elsewhere in Asia, and although the Mongols never made gains in Japan, their invasions exposed weaknesses in the "warrior order."

In the standard account of the invasions, the Mongol-led forces, which included many Chinese and Koreans, attacked the southern island of Kyushu twice. In 1274 and again in 1281 the Japanese warriors met a vastly superior force in terms of troop size, organization, and technology, including the use of explosives. Military historians blamed the so-called traditional form of Japanese combat—announcing one's lineage and engaging in one-on-one combat—for the Japanese losses. The first invasion lasted only a day before a great storm blew the Mongols back into the sea. The Japanese prepared defenses along Hakata Bay, including a wall, and held the Mongols off for several months before another storm came along to save the day. The storms became known as the *divine wind* (*kamikaze*), a term that became popular only in the wartime propaganda of the 1930s and 1940s. During the end of World War II, the Japanese military hoped that a "divine wind" of suicide pilots would prevent a new invasion of another superior, foreign horde—the Americans.

Recent scholarship suggests that the storms might have been a myth. Instead, religious institutions had pushed the divine intervention story in order to accrue rewards for doing their part to defeat the Mongols. Some historians claim that the storms alone could not have defeated the Mongols. So why did the Mongols retreat? Perhaps the Japanese were not outmatched and defeated the Mongols through combative effectiveness. Or the Mongols did indeed overwhelm the Japanese and only wanted to test Japanese military strength, not commit to a full-scale invasion. Kublai was still fighting the Chinese throughout the 1270s and had embarked on invasions elsewhere during the 1280s; he had neither the means nor the inclination to fully invade Japan.

Defending Kyushu and preparing for a third invasion that never came enhanced Hōjō presence in southern and central Japan. The number of military governors in those areas increased, and they were often members of the Hōjō family or its branches. The shogunate recruited men from estates that had been free from any shogunate intervention before the Mongol invasions. Once the shogunate reached into estates not owned by its own vassals, they never again left them alone. Hōjō jurisdiction over major temples and shrines, previously limited to eastern Japan, now extended to those in western Japan as well.

The Mongol invasions did not create new problems for warrior rule; rather, they exacerbated old ones. Many warriors who mobilized their men to defend Kyushu hoped to receive rewards for their efforts. With no national tax or much economic support from the shogunate itself, the burden fell upon those warriors to collect more tax from the lands around them. The Hōjō themselves had few newly acquired lands to hand out, and those who received some rewards were typically warriors in Kyushu. The Hōjō ordered Kyushu families to limit inheritance to male offspring, taking economic prerogatives away from daughters, a practice that, over time, extended to warriors throughout Japan. Gradually, inheritance fell to the oldest son, subordinating even the other male offspring.

The Hōjō also issued a series of prohibitions against warriors selling their land or giving it to nonrelatives. These culminated in a "virtuous edict" that forced anyone who had received land from a warrior family, either as collateral on debts or as commodities sold under the guise of gift giving, to return it to the original warrior families. These debt cancelations were "virtuous" because land was not a commodity to be bought and sold but an inherent part of a warrior clan's heritage. As with other premodern edicts, these were often unclear. Many times, even the beneficiary's claims were unenforceable, and some shrine priests believed the edict applied to them too. Execution and enforcement of the prohibitions were frequently impossible.

Kamakura in decline

Rank-and-file Kamakura vassals and the shogunate suffered from internal disputes during the latter half of the thirteenth century. Two of the Hōjō family's most powerful vassals, Taira Yoritsuna and Adachi Yasumori, began fighting each other after the death of the powerful shogunal regent, Hōjō Tokimune (1284). In 1285, Yoritsuna tried to hunt down Yasumori, which led to a series of murders, purges, and suicides among their supporters and underlings until Yoritsuna himself was killed in 1293. Such violent political intrigues rippled throughout Kyoto, where nobles split into groups of those who resented Hōjō involvement in court politics and those who supported the shogunate. Warrior branch families began breaking off from the main clan by answering the call to defend Kyushu on their own and not simply under the orders of the clan leader. Gradually, warrior clans allied less with their geographically distant kin and more with neighboring warriors.

Adding to the tensions at the top of society, at the bottom there were growing numbers of bandits, pirates, mercenaries, and marauders simply referred to as "evil bands" (*akutō*). Neither the Kamakura shogunate and its vassals nor the court in Kyoto maintained a monopoly over violence in Japan. In the latter half of the thirteenth century these bands of men grew from perhaps a few dozen at most to several hundred. Their numbers peaked during the early fourteenth century, as did their complexity; some even built forts, joined forces with local warriors, or worked for local temples. Many diverse groups of people armed themselves in order to attack the ever-monetizing, commercializing economy of the thirteenth century and to defend themselves against threats from the top of society as well as the bottom.

The legacy of the first warrior regime

Toward the end of the samurai era, in the mid-nineteenth century, warrior pundits linked their existence to Yoritomo's legacy. For them, Yoritomo was a founding father of warrior rule. In general, however, such lavish praise for Yoritomo occurred only late in premodern warrior history. During his lifetime, Yoritomo was not universally well regarded. Yoritomo killed his cousin (Yoshinaka) and his half-brother (Yoshitsune). When Yoritomo wanted to meet the Chinese monk Chin'na Kei, who rebuilt the Todaiji Temple in Kamakura after it burned down in 1180, the monk, repulsed by Yoritomo's violent ways, rebuffed him. When Yoritomo sent him gifts, Chin'na refused to receive them except for a horse saddle and a suit of armor. He donated the saddle to the temple and had the armor melted down and refashioned into nails. Political machinations within the shogunal leadership throughout the late twelfth and thirteenth centuries were violent. Kinsmen remained murder targets; none of Yoritomo's direct descendants died peaceful deaths, and his line did not endure.

The story of Japan's first warrior regime was one of gradual change. Its existence began with the events in Kyoto among the nobility and the emperors. Bureaucratic models, and often the bureaucrats themselves; measures of wealth; patronage of religious institutions; literary conventions; and even marriage politics originated in Kyoto. Whether claiming to be a Minamoto "man," invading noble or temple lands, or using their Kamakura-appointed position to rob locals, warriors had to contend with institutions and customs not of their own creation.

On the other hand, the Kyoto elite could never contain warrior authority. The emperor "bestowed" the title of shogun but that never implied control. Neither Yoritomo nor the Hōjō had to ask to be shogun; they demanded it. At least several Kyoto sovereigns tried to take back warrior power, first with Go-Shirakawa who played Yoritomo against his half-brother Yoshitsune, and again with Go-Toba whose fight against the Hōjō was short-lived. A third emperor, Go-Daigo, succeeded in challenging the shogunate in 1333, but even then the court was unable to check warrior aspirations. Nobles in Kyoto and prominent warriors in Kamakura never completely split into separate realms. After Sanetomo's death in 1219, shoguns came from the Kyoto nobility, not from warrior families.

Legal documents from the Kamakura shogunate speak to the importance of family, broadly defined, which included not only blood relatives but also warrior retainers, nonwarrior servants, nannies and wet nurses, and branch lines distant both geographically and temporally, all of whom could be one's greatest allies or most dangerous enemies. This is true not only of those at the top of warrior society but also among marginal clans, whose desire to persevere and expand could either be threatened or strengthened through military, religious, and noble networks around Japan.

Weak though it might have been, the Kamakura shogunate established a model for subsequent warrior regimes. In 1862, a warrior bureaucrat, complaining about meddling by the Kyoto nobility and their supporters, noted that warriors had been in charge of Japan's politics since the Kamakura shogunate. His boss, Japan's last shogun, eventually surrendered to the emperor in 1868, and a year later a newly formed modern government announced, "Now the evil of misrule by the warriors since the Kamakura period has been overcome and imperial government has been restored."

Chapter 3
War and culture

The sixteenth-century Jesuit Luis Frois described the pirate lord Noshima Murakami as being "so powerful that on these coasts as well as the coastal regions of other kingdoms, all pay him annual tribute out of fear that he will destroy them." His ships continually "flew across the sea." Noshima, like other sixteenth-century warlords, no longer depended on patronage from Kyoto aristocrats to secure wealth, power, and influence. During early warrior history, the centers of power in Kyoto and Kamakura loomed large in the lives of many warriors across Japan, but from the fourteenth to the sixteenth centuries, there was a gradual shift to regional networks, culminating in a century of war in which the "bottom overtook the top" (*gekokujo*).

Warfare was endemic during the three centuries after the fall of the Kamakura shogunate and the Hōjō family in 1331, which affected the relationship between aristocrats and warriors and the nature of warrior wealth and power. Yet, counterintuitively, at the most violent moments in history, warrior support and participation in the art world was also at its height. The sixteenth-century conqueror Oda Nobunaga burned down Buddhist temples and slaughtered thousands of lay supporters, but he also studied Noh theater—performing parts of the play *Atsumori* before embarking on the Battle of Okehazama.

The Kyoto problem

The first crack in Hōjō power since the Jōkyū War (1221) coincided with the rise of yet another emperor, Go-Daigo, who plotted against the Hōjō as Go-Toba did in 1221. Go-Daigo became emperor as a stopgap between the death of the previous emperor, his half-brother, and the ascension of the next one. Unlike those other emperors, however, he was an adult, not an easily controlled child, and he was surrounded by advisors who could support his political aspirations. Not only did he refuse to step down as emperor, which he, the shogunate, and the nobility had agreed would be the case, but he even installed his own son as the next emperor in order to maintain control of Kyoto. He gathered a wide range of supporters, claimed suzerainty over all warriors, and, in 1331, issued a call to arms against the shogunate. The Hōjō quickly put an end to this, exiled him, and purged many of his supporters. Still, not everyone abandoned Go-Daigo's cause. His general, Kusunoki Masashige, kept organizing sympathetic warriors not connected to the shogunate. Go-Daigo promised them titles and wealth just as Yoritomo had done more than a century earlier. Annoyed but confident, the Hōjō sent another army led by Ashikaga Takauji, the newly ascended twenty-eight-year-old head of the Ashikaga clan, longtime powerful Hōjō allies. Instead of fighting Go-Daigo's army, he attacked the shogunate's headquarters in Kyoto. Another Hōjō ally, the Nitta clan, similarly rebelled against the Hōjō in the east. For the first time since the late twelfth century, an emperor finally succeeded in ruling without having to share power with a warrior regime.

But Go-Daigo could not celebrate for long. For three years, from 1333 to 1336, he took control of the shogunate's prerogatives, becoming the sole authority to guarantee warrior appointments and land claims. Meanwhile, however, Takauji's influence grew and Go-Daigo failed to restrain him. Takauji gathered warriors loyal to him as he fought his way to Kamakura to put down a Hōjō resurgence there, and then he fought more enemies on his return trip to Kyoto. Meanwhile, Kyoto erupted in violence. An anonymous author posted complaints about the political situation in Kyoto by the Nijō riverbed: "Things common in the capital these days are night attacks, robbers, counterfeit edicts, criminals, fast horses [to indicate trouble in some place], random fighting, severed heads..."

Like Taira Kiyomori centuries before, Takauji placed his own candidate on the throne in Kyoto, and he began building what would become known as the Muromachi shogunate (1336–1573), named after the district in Kyoto that became the center of his regime. Go-Daigo established his own court just fifty miles south of Kyoto in Yoshino, where he died peacefully. Heirs from both sides fought each other until 1392, when the Yoshino line was crushed, but not forgotten—at the end of World War II, one man claimed to be descended from the southern court and demanded that he replace the northern imposter Hirohito.

The new Ashikaga shogunate depended upon regional warrior families to govern. On the southwest island of Kyushu, where the Mongols tried to invade, military governors essentially ruled as they saw fit. Likewise in the east, around Kamakura, the Ashikaga had to delegate authority to warriors who declared loyalty to them. Though they were never completely independent of shogunal authority, these governors nonetheless gradually assumed rights that their Kamakura predecessors never had: levying taxes, judging and enforcing laws without consulting the shogunate, and collecting fees from local plaintiffs to carry out sentences. With greater revenue, military governors built armies larger than those of the governors of the Kamakura period. Still, not all land in Japan was under the jurisdiction of a military governor. Local strongmen, those not subsumed under the shogunate's bureaucratic purview, also controlled territory. Since many military governors lived in Kyoto and left their provinces to be managed by underlings, strongmen either sought an official title from the shogunate or simply forced the governor to recognize their dominance in the region. The shift to local concerns happened gradually throughout the fifteenth century. For men like the pirate Noshima, regional networks, concerns, and sources of wealth mattered more than ties to the political center in Kyoto. This is the origin of those who would become known as the "great names" (daimyo), the warlords of the sixteenth century.

Tools of warfare

Long before movies depicted samurai wielding lightsaber-sharp swords or charging into battle on mighty horses, warriors themselves enjoyed fantastical descriptions of warrior combat. Warriors and nonwarriors alike read, listened to, and watched performances of "war tales," a genre of writing that had existed since at least the thirteenth century. Historians have cautioned against accepting these tales as accurate portrayals of historical events, but even history textbooks tend to include these problematic literary descriptions of early samurai warfare. The most persistent myth is the belief that warriors announced their family lineages before engaging in battle. It has a wonderful cinematic appeal but is not backed up by historical evidence, and military historians no longer accept it as established practice. A contemporary account of the Mongol invasions describes Japanese warriors who actually tried this, only to be laughed at by the Mongol troops. But these warriors might have simply imitated the heroics described in war tales, in the same way that Japanese Mafioso (*yakuza*) imitate the clothing style featured in Japanese gangster movies.

Nevertheless, warfare was not only about combative effectiveness. Warriors might ignore orders or even target an ally if they felt offended. Warriors painted and decorated their armor not to intimidate but to be noticed as crowds gathered to watch battles unfold. In these battles, killing a lowly rank-and-file soldier did not earn as many accolades as defeating an elite or well-known warrior. In the skirmish tactics of pre-fifteenth-century warfare, some verbal exchanges might have occurred, but that was certainly not the norm.

Early warfare involved armies that were small in comparison to the large-scale warfare of the Warring States era (1477–1590). Samurai vassals might have up to a few dozen men they could bring into battle, but many had only a handful. They could draw on local men as temporary retainers, and, by joining forces with other vassals who served an aristocratic warrior such as Yoritomo, an army could be as small as a few hundred or as many as a few thousand. The first major war, the Gempei War, might have involved several thousand to an unlikely forty thousand troops, depending on the historical source. Given the Gempei War's broad geographical range and the presence of defenses that changed the landscape, like trenches, it is likely that nonwarriors participated as well.

Kamakura-period combat was conducted among warriors on horseback accompanied by men on foot who either fought each other or attempted to unseat mounted warriors. This might seem like an unlikely technique if one imagines the size and speed of modern horses charging through enemy armies. Even Japanese tourists are fascinated by heart-racing demonstrations of mounted shooting (*yabusame*) at shrines around Japan. The archers stand tall above the crowd, galloping at full speed without holding the reins, as they shoot at a series of wooden plank targets. But the premodern reality is a bit less dramatic. Medieval horses in Japan were about the size of a pony, and with an armored man on top, they were hardly fast or durable.

Nonetheless, throughout much of premodern Japanese history, the bow and arrow, not the sword, was the primary weapon of choice for elite warriors. Mounted archery was so common that the phrase "the way of the horse and bow" (*kyūba no michi*) referred to military arts in general. On the early, skirmish-style battlefield, shooting it out against other mounted warriors or picking off footmen were common methods of conducting warfare. Reward petitions and battlefield reports indicate which kinds of weapons were the deadliest. Arrows accounted for most injuries and fatalities up to the fourteenth century. One shot alone usually did not kill warriors, especially wealthier men who could afford decent armor. Not only did the armor itself stop many arrows, but a blanket-like cloth that billowed behind a warrior's armor as he rode away from the enemy could make targeting him difficult by partly obscuring his outline, and it also stopped some of an arrow's momentum. However, with only primitive battlefield medicine, even a stray shot or an unfortunately lodged arrow withdrawn in the wrong way resulted in a slow, sometimes painful death as a warrior bled out.

Swords are another source of fascination for modern audiences, supposedly representing the soul of the samurai and so sharp that they could cut with just a touch. But the sword was merely a sidearm until the fourteenth century, and even then it was used only to gain advantage over an enemy during close-range combat, to finish off a downed opponent, or to decapitate him for later reward. The prototypical sword seen in popular culture was a later invention. Before the Mongol invasions, swords were heavy and had long blades used to attack a horse's leg like a large cleaver. Momentum and weight gave these early swords brute bludgeoning force, making sharpness less important. Extant battle reports and archaeological finds show crushed skulls to be the typical sword fatalities during the medieval period, not subtly delivered cuts to vital arteries.

Besides the iconic sword and bow, weapons included pikes (also referred to as spears), halberds, crossbows, shields, battle axes, large mallets, long rake-like weapons known as "bear claws," and even rocks. Crossbows were common in Chinese armies, and one might expect to find them in Japan. They existed, but perhaps because of their limitations such as slow rate of fire and limited trajectory, they never became popular. Mention of a large crossbow, possibly mounted on a turret, called a "great bow" (*ōyumi*) appears in ancient texts, but no artifacts or even illustrations exist.

The traditional story of how guns came to Japan begins with a Portuguese ship blown by storms onto a small island called Tanegashima. In 1543, so the story goes, the lord of the island realized the importance of the ship's guns and ordered local craftsmen to reverse-engineer them, thus starting a domestic gun-making industry just as the demand for guns spiked during a time of national war. Military historians in Japan have noted that primitive harquebuses, early matchlock guns with ball ammunition loaded from the front, entered Japan as early as the mid-fifteenth century from Okinawa, Southeast Asia, and China. The Europeans did not introduce arms to Japan, but they brought large quantities and probably better-quality weapons during the latter half of the sixteenth century. Guns could make the difference in battle, although they did not change the essential nature or tactics of warfare in Japan.

The biggest myth told about guns in Japan is that the samurai eventually abandoned them in favor of the sword because the sword was more honorable and represented the soul of the samurai. This is simply not true. First, people continued to use guns in the few, small-scale battles and uprisings during the otherwise peaceful era that followed the Warring States period. Lords gave them as gifts, and commoners and warriors alike used guns in hunting and for recreation. From the seventeenth to the early nineteenth centuries, cannons positioned at Japan's largest port, Nagasaki, were equivalent to those used in Europe. And samurai used guns against Chinese accused of smuggling in the southern port of Nagasaki. Thus, warriors never "gave up" guns; they still used them. But the opportunities to use them dwindled after the Warring States period.

The archetypical samurai armor has a long history, but like weapons, it changed over time. Armor from the Kamakura period (1180–1333) consisted of pieces of lacquered wood woven together, with some metal reinforcement on the chest. It covered most of the body except for the face but did not protect the extremities well. This type of full armor was expensive, and most foot soldiers wore nothing more than basic armor that covered the torso. Chain mail, like the European version but made with smaller chains, was used from the fourteenth century onward and was combined with an older style of armor made of metal plates. Helmets varied depending on the status of the warrior. They were made from a range of materials that included iron, steel, metal plates riveted together, and hardened leather for common soldiers. Armor changed to reflect shifts in battle tactics, especially during the fifteenth and sixteenth centuries, when war was conducted at a much larger scale with better organized units of men attacking with pikes, volleys of arrows, and guns. Immaculately preserved armor can be found in museums throughout North America and Europe, but most of these pieces date to the seventeenth through nineteenth centuries when there was little warfare, and armor was either worn in warrior processions or simply displayed in the home, seeing no combat at all. There are occasional echoes of European influence in Japanese armor, such as helmets shaped like those worn by European counterparts, but those are rare.

Japanese warriors did not use European-style, single-handed shields. Japanese shields were typically as tall as a man and were made of wood. They often included a stand so that a line of men could move and place them side by side to create a movable wall. Often these were impromptu defenses of opportunity: wooden doors, portions of walls, or tatami woven flooring ripped from buildings during battle.

And what of castles? There are two issues that might disappoint. First, castles as Westerners imagine them, with moats and walls surrounding a central keep, were a relatively late development in Japanese history, dating to the sixteenth century at the earliest. Some castles supposedly have earlier origins, but those were rebuilt several times after the Warring States era. During earlier times, such as the Gempei War, some fortifications existed, but nothing grand or permanent. Warriors who served the Kamakura shogunate might have had a large compound with walls and several buildings at most. Since many warriors worked as managers, police, and governors, there was little need to build large structures. Even Yoritomo's Kamakura palace, which housed many of the shogunate's offices, no longer exists.

Only in the sixteenth century did the Japanese build castles designed to keep an enemy out and to confound him should he penetrate the outer defenses. Despite the stylistic difference with European castles, they shared many features: moats, sturdily built narrow gates to keep enemies from flooding in, and small windows that allowed warriors to shoot arrows or pour boiling liquid onto intruding forces. The biggest difference between European and Japanese castles was the walls. Although their construction changed to accommodate the introduction of guns into Japan, these walls nonetheless did not suffer from punishing, artillery-led sieges as did their European counterparts. The greatest threat to the integrity of Japanese walls was earthquakes. To provide some protection from them, the walls were not built vertically straight using stones stuck together with mortar. Instead, Japanese walls had a slight curve, and builders cut and stacked stones to fit perfectly, filling gaps with smaller stones, without the need for mortar.

Although there are many castles throughout Japan today, only a dozen of them have keeps older than a hundred years. Keeps rarely served a military function; they were used mostly to project authority across the landscape. Fires throughout the Tokugawa period (1600–1868) destroyed many keeps and other wooden structures such as watchtowers or guard posts. Since keeps look

4. A full set of armor from the eighteenth century imitates the style of the twelfth to thirteenth centuries, illustrating how warriors of later periods idealized their medieval forerunners. Many museum armor pieces are in excellent condition because they were not used in combat but displayed in warriors' homes.

5. Himeji Castle, a UNESCO World Heritage site, is one of the largest and oldest castles in Japan. Originally constructed in the fourteenth century, it was partially built and rebuilt after the warlord Toyotomi Hideyoshi took it over in the late sixteenth century. Like many Japanese castles, it was used by the Japanese military during World War II.

impressive, they have been added to castles that never originally featured one. Local politicians have realized that castles are big tourist attractions and symbols of civic pride. Most of the castles in Japan are post–World War II fabrications that accompanied the postwar economic boom. Some of the reconstructions are inaccurately built or use too much concrete, giving castles a shiny but inauthentic look.

The most "authentic" castle is probably Himeji Castle, a UNESCO World Heritage site. Himeji survived the fate suffered by other castles that were either torn down after the Meiji Restoration (1868) and sold for scrap, destroyed by natural disasters, or bombed by the United States during World War II. However, even Himeji has undergone repairs and has been criticized by some as being much whiter than it would have been before the twentieth century. Nonetheless, Himeji is considered the archetypal Japanese castle, and many castle reconstructions have been modeled after Himeji regardless of the historical differences.

The warrior in combat

For much of Japanese history, compensation was the key to obtaining service from warriors. Yoritomo's success hinged on his ability to reward allies, the Hōjō lost support when they could not deliver enough rewards to those who fought the Mongols, and Emperor Go-Daigo was able to buy samurai away from the last enemy general who tried to fight him in 1333. So how did warriors prove their service? By submitting reports and petitions for rewards, and collecting evidence—namely, heads.

Taking heads had its origins in police duties. Early warrior violence primarily involved chasing down criminals and decapitating them to prove that the execution had been carried out. Heads would be collected, tagged, and publicly exhibited around Kyoto. During larger battles, headhunting functioned as a way for warriors to record their achievements and thus receive payment for their service. Heads would be cleaned and displayed on a board for a general to examine. Well-known enemies earned them the highest rewards, but differentiating middle- and lower-ranking warriors could be trickier; prisoners helped identify heads. Heads from common soldiers were typically ignored.

The downside of beheading an enemy during battle is obvious; a warrior could be killed while taking a head. Some generals solved this problem by issuing "cut and toss" orders, which tended to rely on eyewitness accounts of the beheading, thus skipping the collection side of the process. Warriors also gamed the system by scouring the battlefield for wounded men who were not yet dead, beheading noncombatants, forging or switching nameplates, and looking for abandoned heads, activities that were deemed unseemly and worthy of ridicule.

No notions of honor, rooted in maintaining a reputation, trumped the desire to emerge victorious. There were no written codes of conduct, no tactics deemed unacceptable. These included arson, which killed indiscriminately, and ambushes and night attacks, when the enemy was caught unaware. Trickery, particularly clever trickery, could earn a warrior praise, such as the following from a sixteenth-century military chronicle titled *The Military Mirror of Kai*:

> During the Battle of Toishikuzure there was an enemy separated from his comrades and armed with a long spear. When Imai chased after him, the enemy, a warrior of the warlord Uesugi Kenshin, changed the position of his spear and was going to strike Imai from his horse. Because the enemy was walking he could move about freely, but Imai was on a horse and could not. Imai, famed warrior that he was, tricked his opponent by calling out to him as if he were an ally. As the enemy lowered his spear to greet him, Imai's men moved in to attack. Imai is a martial expert even though he was not adept with a sword and did not know much about martial arts.

There are few details about how warriors trained together in groups during the Kamakura period. But we know that training was a social activity that helped develop some degree of group identity. During the Kamakura period, men used hunting as an opportunity to learn group coordination. Warrior managers on estates had portions of land reserved for hunting or falconry, which helped warriors learn how to survey terrain. Ceremonial shooting from horseback began among warriors in Kyoto in the eleventh century at the latest, but the tactic is often associated with Kamakura, where Yoritomo held shooting events at large shrines. Dog shooting was another activity that was recreational, social, and useful for military preparedness. Professional dog handlers kept and released dogs into an enclosed area while warriors shot at them from horseback with blunted arrows.

6. An early fourteenth-century hand scroll scene depicts the Battle at Rokuhara, when the Minamoto clan attacked Taira Kiyomori's base at Rokuhara palace. The Minamoto lost both the battle and the Heiji Rebellion (1160). Here, two Taira men descend on a Minamoto warrior, pulling him back to decapitate him.

Training and ritual often occurred in Buddhist and Shinto spaces, and thus, warfare and religion intertwined. Buddhist temples and Shinto shrines wielded political, military, and economic power. They possessed land, collected taxes, lent money (with interest rates as high as 300 percent), and provided protection for a variety of merchant guilds, including alcohol (sake) and weapon production. The notion that there were white-scarfed "warrior monks" armed with glaives (*naginata*) derives mostly from art history, literature, and popular culture. However, monks whose previous career included military experience continued to fight on behalf of temples. Major temples could rely on lay supporters, sometimes retired warriors, who acted as an institution's "muscle." They helped collect loans or protected the temples from bandits, pirates, and warriors who intruded on their estates.

Religious institutions confronted their enemies with supernatural weapons; prayers and chanting were more akin to spell-casting than prostrations for good luck. Clerics expected to be rewarded for calling upon the gods and Buddhas for the "divine winds" that they claimed destroyed the invading Mongol forces. Warriors had Sanskrit words inscribed on their weapons and armor to protect them from harm. The invocations and imagery of esoteric Buddhism mattered more than Zen meditation to a warrior heading into combat. They read about, or learned from other warriors and monks, spells such as this one that told the chanter how to escape from an attack by fire: "To escape from an enemy who attacks you with fire, face the direction of water, or at the sky, and chant 'praise to the god of rain and water' seven times. Then incant '*on, su'u ruinō ten sowaka*' and pour water down a bow from its top."

Warriors also paid homage to divine beings associated with war. This included the Buddhist god-like Marishiten, who carried an assortment of weapons in her six hands while riding atop a wild boar, and Hachiman, another Buddhist god of war. Deities appeared in dreams and could portend positive results in war. Some warrior hegemons promoted their rule as divinely ordained or were promoted as gods by their followers after death.

An era of war

The fifteenth and sixteenth centuries saw an interesting mix of warfare and high culture. During the latter half of the fifteenth century, the most influential warrior clans, including the Ashikaga, suffered from internal succession disputes that became violent. Even after those conflicts burned through Kyoto over the course of a decade, the rest of Japan experienced a new kind of warfare fundamentally different from anything it had experienced before. Battles were no longer conducted under the logic of chasing down enemies in the name of punishing rebels (Gempei War) or uppity emperors (Jōkyū War); warriors fought to expand and defend territory.

Like previous wars, the Ōnin War (1467–77) originated from the structural tensions at the political top. Three warrior clans, the Hosokawa, Hatakeyama, and Shiba, served as military governors but also rotated among themselves a newly created position during the Muromachi shogunate known as a "deputy shogun." After the death of the third shogun, Yoshimitsu (died 1408), the subsequent shoguns no longer had the ability or influence to control the shogunate on their own. Nor was there a single family like the Hōjō, connected to the shogun via marriage, powerful enough to dominate. Therefore, the deputy shogun and his family cooperated with the other clans to maintain stability in the shogunate. It was an efficient system when the clans were internally cohesive and interacted well. Their rivalry ensured that no single clan dominated. But when the clans were not strong or when tensions arose among the deputy shogun families, the shogunate weakened. Disputes that broke out within these families were tied to issues of who would control the shogunate at any given moment. Moreover, military governors, in what was a temporary post with little authority during the Kamakura era, gradually began to function as semi autonomous lords.

It was easy to dismiss the Ashikaga clan entirely after the death of its last, great leader, the third shogun, Yoshimitsu. Even after he retired he still controlled the shogunate through his son, the fourth shogun. Warriors, nobles, and even the Ming Chinese respected Yoshimitsu, but they despised his son. The fifth shogun died young, and the sixth shogun, Yoshinori, who showed some real ability to rule, was deemed too tyrannical by many of the important military families, and for good reason: cooks who underperformed, gardeners who broke a tree branch on a plum tree, fifty-nine members of the nobility, and even some warriors were killed, purged, or fled for their lives from his wrath. The military governor Akamatsu Mitsuhide brutally assassinated Yoshinori after learning that Yoshinori might take land from him and give it to someone else. Mitsuhide held a party in his villa on the outskirts of Kyoto and invited Yoshinori and other prominent warriors to partake in a favorite warrior pastime, viewing Noh theater. Horses suddenly rushed through the gardens, creating a distraction and allowing the assassins to break in and decapitate Yoshinori. A courtier at the time wrote that Yoshinori "died like a dog."

His son, the seventh shogun, died in childhood, so the shogun's position passed to another son, the much-maligned Yoshimasa. Although Yoshimasa represented the height of warrior involvement in noble culture—he was an accomplished poet—he was an indecisive shogun who had just enough influence in the shogunate to destroy it. Wanting to retire and having failed to produce an heir, he asked his brother Yoshimi to take over the shogun position. He planned to formally adopt his brother, a common solution for warriors who needed to secure an heir when no biological son was forthcoming. Yoshimi, quite rightly, was suspicious; what if Yoshimasa's wife suddenly gave birth to a son? And besides, Yoshimi, like other noble sons no longer in line to become head of the family, was happily ensconced in an unrelated career—in his case, as a Buddhist abbot. Unfortunately for everyone involved, after Yoshimi accepted his brother's offer,

Yoshimasa's wife gave birth to a son. The various supporters of Yoshimi and his newborn nephew battled it out in Kyoto, exacerbating an already volatile situation that grew into the Ōnin War.

The fighting of the Ōnin War signaled a shift toward a new kind of combat. Although some of the fighting occurred in the countryside, most of it took place inside the city of Kyoto itself. It represented neither the earlier logic of hunting criminals and rebels nor the engagement of participants in open field combat. Defensive blocks of men armed with pikes proved better suited to urban warfare than mounted warriors. Fighting occurred haphazardly in yards, gardens, and streets by those who were not warriors as such, but commoners recruited to fill the ranks of otherwise small armies. The purpose was simply to defeat an enemy and, in many cases, to exact revenge. In previous wars, when an elite opponent was not decapitated, he would be allowed to retire in exile. But during the Ōnin War, violence was so intense that some warriors made cups from an enemy's lacquered skull. The war was so devastating that when a reporter asked the seventeenth head of the Hosokawa family, Hosokawa Morisada, father of Prime Minister Hosokawa Morihiro (1993–94), about his family's legacy, Morisada replied, "Yes, our family used to have many excellent treasures but they burned up during the War." The reporter thought that "the War" referred to World War II, but Morisada clarified, "Oh, by 'the War' I mean the Ōnin War."

The shogunate itself never fully recovered, and warriors who remained in the countryside began to assert themselves against their neighbors, rivals, and absentee superiors. With Kyoto destroyed, many of its residents flooded out of the city to the growing number of castle towns being erected around Japan. Military governors who focused their energies on regional bases continued to maintain power locally, but others with little or no connection to prominent warrior families fought to obtain and secure territory. Contemporaries invoked Chinese history to describe the era as a time of "warring states," referring to the conflicts in antiquity immediately before the founding of imperial China. Skill in warfare alone was not enough; warlords needed to monopolize trade, encourage commerce, increase income, and attract noble-born literate men from Kyoto to establish laws that helped them pacify the realm. No potential alliance was overlooked as they gathered warriors, mercenaries, and noncombatant supporters to serve them.

It is no wonder that a Jesuit missionary writing to his brethren in Europe referred to these warlords as "kings." Domains were neither states nor kingdoms, but a warlord wielded authority in his realm with little regard for the shogunate, a far cry from the pre–Ōnin War military governors.

"The bottom overthrowing the top" was a phrase used at the time to describe the phenomenon of relatively unknown aspirants taking control of a domain or carving out a slice of land on their own. Even warlords with an impressive lineage were not guaranteed victory. The Ōuchi family, which had once supported the Ashikaga during the conflict between the Northern and Southern Courts, was one such prominent clan that fell into obscurity. They dominated southern Japan and ruled their coastal domain from a castle town called Yamaguchi. There they accrued wealth from trade with nearby Korea and China and, eventually, European traders who began arriving in Japan during the sixteenth century. At one point, Yamaguchi became so economically dynamic that it rivaled Kyoto itself, and the Ōuchi even planned to move the emperor permanently to Yamaguchi. Eventually, however, the Ōuchi were overthrown by one of their vassal clans, the Mōri, and Yamaguchi collapsed, never to regain its former glory.

The shogunate remained a potential source of legitimacy for warlords like Oda Nobunaga (1534–82). Nobunaga was the first of three warlords to conquer large swaths of territory and pacify the country. Nobunaga's rise to power illustrates how a warlord took

7. Portraits of warriors usually show them clean-shaven and without much facial expression. This Shibata clan warrior appears mischievous in this iconoclastic sixteenth-century portrait that signifies a time when the upheaval of warfare allowed people to overturn aesthetic norms.

advantage of upheaval. His family, the Oda, were only minor warrior vassals serving the Shiba, a branch of the Ashikaga clan. The Shiba rotated the deputy shogun position with the Hosokawa and the Hatekeyama, and like them, the Shiba were weakened from internal family disputes of the sort that characterized the Ōnin War and were unable to control warriors in their provincial lands. The Oda, who carried out mundane functions in the province on behalf of the absentee Shiba, overthrew the Shiba and took over the province.

Nobunaga inherited titles and land from his father, but he had to spend many years securing control over the Oda clan. As was true throughout warrior history, family members were targets—Nobunaga killed his brother. He also negotiated with local influential men in the province, a necessary strategy because the province, Owari, was centrally located, close to Kyoto, and agriculturally productive. A combination of political alliances, strategic and tactical skills, and Nobunaga's ability to incorporate the men of his defeated enemies drove his success. Eventually he attracted support from the shogun Ashikaga Yoshiaki. The two men needed each other. Yoshiaki required Nobunaga's military might, and Nobunaga wanted the legitimizing approval of the shogun regardless of how weak the shogunate might have become. But Nobunaga never accepted titles from the shogun. Doing so would have made him the shogun's subordinate and complicated Nobunaga's ambitions. As with the Hōjō and Go-Toba in 1221, and Ashikaga Takauji and Go-Shirakawa during the 1330s, Nobunaga was forced to defend himself against an older institution of rule, using force to do so.

Nobunaga probably did not set out to destroy the political relevance of the shogun and his regime, but relations between the two men waned. Yoshiaki sought help from Nobunaga's rivals, including the powerful warlord Takeda Shingen who, like Nobunaga, had successfully conquered large swaths of territory. Nobunaga, in turn, sent Yoshiaki a list of complaints about the shogun's behavior. Eventually the shogun declared war on Nobunaga in 1573, and despite Nobunaga's offers of peace, he lost patience with Yoshiaki, who fled Kyoto, never to return. Nobunaga defeated Yoshiaki's coalition and ordered the beheading of the shogun's top three warlords—he then had their heads lacquered and painted in gold dust to show to the troops.

Nobunaga eliminated his final enemy, institutional Buddhism, over the course of the next several years, killing tens of thousands of adherents of the True Pure Land faith, including commoner men and women. In so doing, he forever eliminated Buddhism as an institution of rule. For more than five hundred years, major temples had enjoyed patronage from the Kyoto aristocracy and warrior elites. After Nobunaga's campaign, temples no longer maintained armies or possessed the wealth they once did. In 1582, the court, which had supported him since his victory over the shogun, offered him the title of shogun. But before he could accept, one of his own generals, Akechi Mitsuhide, attacked him, cornering him and his son in a temple. Wounded and clearly defeated, both Nobunaga and his heir committed suicide after ordering that their bodies be burned. Nobunaga's career ended as it had started, in the constant "bottom overthrowing the top" that defined the times.

Nobunaga had conquered about a third of Japan, established policies to encourage trade, and amassed a sizable army, but, as with any warlord, the issue arose as to who would inherit that legacy. His remaining son, Nobutaka, was far from Kyoto when news arrived that his father and older brother had been killed. He blamed his cousin for the betrayal, as kinsmen were the usual suspects in prominent warrior families. He was forced aside, leaving one of Nobunaga's generals, Hideyoshi, to avenge Nobunaga and take control of his forces.

Nobunaga exemplified one type of Warring States story, a vassal family usurping their patrons. Hideyoshi represented another type, an individual of obscure, lowly origins who rose through the ranks. He and his early biographers cultivated this image; he told foreigners that a ray of sunlight had entered his mother's womb, indicating divine birth. In other words, he used both sides of the classic hero story—the everyman of humble beginnings and also divine birth that would lead to heavenly ordained greatness. At any rate, he built on Nobunaga's gains and secured alliance, obedience, and dominance from warlords across Japan. He accomplished this by fielding the largest army in the world at the time, as many as two hundred thousand men, much larger than any contemporaneous European army. He personally owned 12 percent of Japan, including some of the largest cities, such as Kyoto, and the major ports that handled lucrative trade from China, Korea, and European merchants.

We should not attribute Hideyoshi's successes to his abilities alone; the warlords themselves were willing to acquiesce to his policies so that they could block threats from within their domains. After all, only a few decades before Hideyoshi's unification, the vassal family Mōri had overthrown their lords, the Ōuchi. The final decades of the late sixteenth century and early years of the seventeenth are a story of preventing the types of upheaval that many of these warlords themselves took advantage of. For example, warriors were removed from villages to keep them from building local power bases independent of the warlord's authority. Hideyoshi tried to disarm villagers knowing that local people posed a significant threat to his conquest over Japan. They sometimes created egalitarian leagues of farmers, merchants, mercenaries, militant monks, and other "nonwarriors" who nonetheless armed themselves and fought collectively. *Warrior* was still an ambiguous term. Often there was no clear distinction between who counted as a warrior and who did not. People of all statuses joined together to form leagues that protected their members against warlords with large armies. An attack on one member of a league prompted a response from them all, something like a premodern Japanese North Atlantic Treaty

Organization. Geographic proximity or even a shared religious affiliation was enough to justify collective defense.

Hideyoshi solidified his conquest in 1590, but his vision extended beyond Japan to China, and he started what became the largest war in premodern world history, the Imjin War (1592–98). Not long after Hideyoshi had unified Japan, he sent messengers to European representatives in Asia: the Spanish governor of the Philippines and the Portuguese stationed in their colony of Goa, now a state in India. They responded with a mix of confusion and minimal acknowledgment of this man whom they had never heard of before, but Hideyoshi took their response as recognition of his greatness. Such was the extent of Hideyoshi's confidence. He asked the Korean king to allow him access to the peninsula to make way for his armies that would conquer China. The Koreans demurred, and in 1592 Hideyoshi ordered warlords, mostly from the south, to lead their samurai to Korea.

Many have speculated about why Hideyoshi invaded Korea. Some have argued that he wanted to keep the warlords and their samurai busy to prevent a revolt. Although this is not a consensus view, it has one element of truth—namely, that Hideyoshi liked to move warlords around to keep them occupied and their resources strapped. Others believe that he wanted to rid himself of Christian warlords. Nearly a quarter of a million Japanese had converted to Christianity since Catholic missionaries had arrived in the latter half of the sixteenth century. Most conversions occurred in the southwest, on the island of Kyushu, where missionaries first landed as they traveled north along maritime routes from South and Southeast Asia (earning them the name, in Japan, of "southern barbarians"). Many warlords sent to Korea were among the converts.

Initially the Imjin War went well for the Japanese. Nearly 158,000 men, at least twice as many as in any European army, invaded from the south and made it to the northern capital in a few weeks.

For the Korean kingdom of Choson, it was the perfect storm: the Koreans' military organization was not good, the peninsula had been at relative peace for centuries, and now they were facing battle-seasoned Japanese. The Korean king called upon his patron, the Ming Chinese emperor, who sent a small force. Initially, the emperor had not felt threatened by the Japanese—until the first army he dispatched was wiped out. Eventually he sent an army of approximately one hundred thousand. Chinese support and the Korean naval successes under Admiral Yi Sunsin, who cut off Korea-based troops from Japan, forced the Japanese to retreat. For several years Hideyoshi engaged in peace talks with the Ming, during which time some Japanese soldiers gave up arms and blended into local Korean communities or defected to the Ming army. Finally, shortly before dying of illness, Hideyoshi gave the order to retreat completely; the warlords were all too happy to comply.

The war devastated Korea, which took centuries to recover. In the modern period, the Imjin War became the first historical source of tension between Korea and Japan. Attempts to rectify this tension have failed. In Kyoto, for instance, there is a national historical site called "Ear Mound," which is a bit misleading; twenty thousand Korean noses were buried there. Warriors had brought them back to Japan, instead of decapitated heads, for reward. During the 1990s, there was a campaign by South Koreans and Kyoto city officials to remove the mound and send its contents to South Korea for proper burial. But Japan's central government denied the request because it was designated a national cultural asset.

Until recently, Chinese scholars have downplayed the war's impact on Ming China. After all, Japanese warriors never made it to China. But the Ming emperor committed enough resources to the "Korean campaign," as it was known in China, that it drained Ming coffers. This made it more difficult for the Chinese ruler to

8. During the invasions of Korea, Japanese warriors collected the ears and noses of enemy troops and civilians as trophies. Previously known as Hanazuka (Nose Mound), Mimizuka (Ear Mound) symbolizes the Japanese invasions of the Korean peninsula in both the premodern and the modern periods and is dedicated to the souls of the maimed individuals.

put down rebellions from within China and fight enemies to the north.

Japanese warlords brought back with them Korean slaves, especially artisans and intellectuals. Among them were potters who were forced to establish Korean ceramic workshops in Japan. In fact, Hideyoshi's invasion was also called the "pottery war." Why did daimyo want intellectuals and potters? What was the connection between warfare and culture?

Warrior "values"

From the beginning, elite warriors depended upon connections to Kyoto that required some degree of cultural literacy. A significant number of shoguns during the Kamakura era came from Kyoto noble families with no military identity as such. Warrior regimes in Kamakura and then in Kyoto, as well as small local governments, drew talent from middling noble families. Thus it should be no surprise that elite, literate warriors participated in and patronized art in its many forms—from art collecting and poetry writing to the funding of Buddhist temples, statues, and religious artwork. The city of Kamakura even had its own Zen Buddhist temple system that mirrored the one in Kyoto.

For warriors with court rank ambitions, writing was essential for interacting with elite nobility and clergy. But we should not think of poetry in the modern sense of the term—as a leisure activity, a pastime with no function beyond observations about contemporary society. Poetry in premodern Japan could be used to comment on current events, but more important, poetry demonstrated one's knowledge of classical Chinese and Japanese literature. Good writing, in content and in form—handwriting mattered—was a means for noblemen in Kyoto to climb the career ladder. The monk Jien exchanged poetry with Yoritomo, which led to a mutually beneficial relationship; Jien needed to secure rights for his estate and Yoritomo wanted information from him. People also wrote poetry together as a social activity, linking one poem to another; an elite warrior could expose himself to public humiliation if he failed to write adequately.

As warriors took up permanent residence in Kyoto during the Muromachi period, they deferred to courtier sensibilities. They intensified the adoption of aristocratic culture into their own families, using Chinese learning when creating their own clan rules, and forming a parallel set of warrior etiquette that mimicked aristocratic traditions. In other words, nascent warrior culture and identity had its roots in noble culture.

One text that imparts what it meant to be a proper warrior is a letter purportedly written during the early fifteenth century by a military governor, Imagawa Ryōshun, to his son. It emphasizes the importance of nonmilitary learning, respect for the clan over the individual, and the way to manage a clan and its properties. The text was not written in a historical vacuum; some themes had appeared in earlier warrior texts for elites. Buddhist notions of the respect for life and Confucian ideas about proper behavior when interacting with others punctuate Imagawa's letter, as they did many early East Asian writings. The Imagawa "house code" includes these precepts:

- As you do not understand the arts of peace, your skill in the arts of war will not, in the end, achieve victory.
- You like to roam about, hawking and cormorant-fishing, relishing the purposeless taking of life.
- To build your own dwelling, you razed the pagoda and other buildings of the memorial temple of our ancestors.
- You permit yourself to forget the kindness that our lord and father showed us; thus you destroy the principles of loyalty and filial piety.
- You disregard other people's viewpoints; you bully them and rely on force.
- You excel at drinking bouts, amusements, and gambling, but you forget the business of our clan.
- Expertise in the military arts and warfare are the way of the warrior. What first makes him distinguished is the capacity for management.
- It appears clearly from the Four Books [of Confucianism], the Five Classics [of China], and military texts that he who can only defend his territory but has no learning cannot govern well.

These precepts did not necessarily apply to lower-ranking warriors but to elite men like Imagawa. Only the upper echelons of the warrior community had access to an education that allowed them to read the Chinese classics (in fact, familiarity with Chinese philosophy can help the modern student of samurai history understand warrior ideals). During the fifteenth and sixteenth centuries, military governors and warlords used Imagawa's letter in their own clans and adopted it to create similar teachings. The Imagawa letter reached the peak of its popularity during the Tokugawa period (1600–1868), an age of peace when warrior education focused on management and civil learning, not military skill.

Warrior thought is also reflected in the teachings of Hōjō Sōun, a fifteenth-century warrior loyal to the Imagawa clan during the Warring States era. He was not directly related to the Hōjō clan of the Kamakura period (1185–1333) but consciously adopted the surname in order to inherit their powerful legacy—warriors idealized the past. His teachings spread throughout all warrior ranks in the lands he controlled, including such aphorisms as these:

- Rise early in the morning. If you wake up late your servants will be negligent and they will be of no use to you. Your public and private affairs will go into disarray. Your lord will forsake you. Think carefully about this.
- Do not think that you should have fine swords and clothes like others have. Just be sure they do not appear slovenly; that's enough. You'll be ridiculed if you borrow what you don't have or spend too much effort on such things.
- In seeking good friends, find those who are good at writing and learning in general. Bad friends to exclude are those who play *go*, *shogi* [a form of chess], the flute or the *shakuhachi* [an end-blown bamboo flute]. It is not a shame to be ignorant of those pursuits. These are simply ways to pass the idle time. The good and bad of a man is determined by the friends he keeps. [Then, quoting the *Analects* of Confucius,] "When three men walk together, among them, I have teachers. I choose to follow what is good about the good man, and learn to better myself from the bad man."

- Of course you should know the ways of culture [*bun*] and war [*bu*], along with the military arts [literally, "bow and horse"]; there is no need to write more about this. From antiquity it has been the rule that civil culture is on the left and military learning is on the right; one must practice both.

Sōun also has much to say about how to serve one's lord: always show respect to one's seniors, follow orders to the letter and without delay, and maintain one's residence. Like the Imagawa letter, Sōun's writing deems civil arts to be just as important as the martial arts.

Warriors in Kyoto culture

During the Muromachi period, warriors also began entering the Kyoto artistic realm not of their own making: the world of art collecting, connoisseurship, and performance. The intertwining of politics and art intensified with the Ashikaga presence in Kyoto. Even the relatively uninitiated, like Oda Nobunaga, could not resist the social and political gains to be made by engaging the nobility and wealthy commoners through art.

What we might today think of as "traditional" Japanese culture, such as Noh theater or the tea ceremony, expanded during an era of war and benefited from warrior patronage. These activities became new fields of knowledge as artists themselves created new types of networks by interacting with the nobility and warrior patrons. Theater had long existed in Japan, but we know few details about it until it became an artistic field of knowledge, written about and codified as "Noh," during the fourteenth and fifteenth centuries. That is, there were no texts that attempted to define theatrical standards, training, or aesthetics. It was only when Zeami, regarded as the creator of Noh, received patronage from the third Ashikaga shogun, Yoshimitsu, that he had connections to intellectuals who provided him with the education and vocabulary to elevate theater from entertainment to high art.

Noh played to its newfound audience; many performances featured warrior heroes, drawing from the classic *Tale of Heike*.

Art had a practical function; warriors gained access to social networks among nonwarriors through cultural activities. Only after spending time in Kyoto, with nobles, did Nobunaga start practicing *kemari* (often referred to as kickball but closer to hacky sack). Nobles and even Kamakura shoguns hired kemari teachers to improve their game, and other elite warriors wanted to become involved. Likewise, art collecting allowed warriors to mingle with the wealthy and to form alliances with other warriors through gift-giving or by bestowing rewards on subordinates.

The tea ceremony was among the iconic aristocratic pastimes that moved into the warrior sphere and eventually came to represent it. The tea ceremony combined two activities: collecting and connoisseurship with physical practice. Tea gatherings began as social events where rare objects could be displayed, perhaps as a part of other day-long events such as poetry writing or even gaming. But gradually it became an intimate affair when a few men of varying social classes gathered in a small, unassuming room where attention centered on the host, who would prepare the tea for his guests. Here too, Nobunaga is often regarded as the first prominent warrior who engaged in this practice, keeping two well-known tea experts on his payroll, including Sen no Rikyū, the first tea master to write extensively about tea aesthetics and whose teachings are followed even today.

Hideyoshi, like other warriors, took his cultural cues from Nobunaga. He continued to employ Rikyū, relying on him almost as a collaborator. Rikyū helped Hideyoshi set up tea gatherings, display tea-related objects, and learn the aesthetics of tea as defined and redefined by Rikyū. Hideyoshi even held a large open-air tea event, inviting anyone, regardless of status, to attend. But the constantly changing world of tea clashed with warrior desire to impose order; those who did not attend the event were forbidden to participate in future communal tea gatherings. One can imagine the tension between a hegemon with designs on conquering China and his tea master who was regarded as a cultural icon.

As an indication of his importance, Rikyū oversaw the installation of a statue of himself over the gate of an important Zen temple. This was regarded as an insult to Hideyoshi, who might pass under Rikyū's feet. In 1591 Hideyoshi ordered Rikyū to kill himself. After writing a death poem and piercing his abdomen with a short sword, he was shown the mercy of decapitation by a warrior in attendance. Whatever reasons Hideyoshi might have had for executing Rikyū, the tea master nonetheless represented a challenge to Hideyoshi's authority in the world beyond politics and war—people obeyed Hideyoshi but they listened to Rikyū.

Chapter 4
Warriors in an age of peace

The samurai loom large in the scholarship of the Tokugawa period (1600–1868), also known as the Edo period or simply "early modern Japan." Despite being known as a time when commoners wrote and produced knowledge more than ever before, when commoner urban popular culture eclipsed the Kyoto-centric highbrow culture, samurai remained central to macro historical analysis. For some types of history, especially diplomatic and political histories, this makes sense; samurai rule achieved its peak during the Tokugawa period. Nobunaga eliminated institutional religion as a political, economic, and military force even though religion, broadly conceived, helped legitimize and promote political action. And until the very end of the Tokugawa period, the nobility and emperors in Kyoto no longer had the authority they once did. They depended on the shogun's largess and sent ambassadors to the Tokugawa shogunate headquartered in the city of Edo (modern Tokyo). No emperor even considered challenging the warrior regime during the Tokugawa period.

Scholars of economic, institutional, intellectual, religious, and cultural history all address the role samurai played in either constraining or fostering changes in early modern society. One could even argue that the real age of the samurai began in the Tokugawa period. Some historians have depicted this as a dark time, when a putatively rigid status system kept commoners in their place, denying them access to the decision-making processes at the top and condemning them to physical toil at the bottom. Others see this as a relatively bright era when health and standard of living were generally good compared to European countries at the time. Likewise, popular culture, literature, art, and theater are viewed as either sites of resistance against or vehicles for escape from the pressures of warrior rule. In comparative East Asian history, Japan is considered either similar to China and Korea because they all underwent bureaucratization at roughly the same time, or as fundamentally different because Japan was ruled by warriors, unlike its neighbors.

Tokugawa Ieyasu represented the last generation of warlords who experienced a life of war; after the early 1600s they were simply "lords." The Matsudaira clan, Ieyasu's birth family, gave him as a child hostage to the Imagawa clan in exchange for help fighting against the Oda; hostages and marriage were the two methods for securing alliances among warlords. But he was kidnapped en route and handed over to the Oda, with whom he lived for several years. He returned to the Imagawa during a hostage exchange involving one of the Oda sons. This might sound like a rough childhood, but he was scarcely mistreated; he received an education under the Imagawa, led armies on their behalf, and married an Imagawa woman.

Ieyasu lived with the Imagawa until they were defeated by the Oda, after which he returned to his homeland and took control of the Matsudaira. He became Nobunaga's ally and, eventually, his vassal. Nobunaga trusted Ieyasu, and for good reason. When Ieyasu was forced to decide between maintaining his alliance with Nobunaga or killing his own wife and son under Nobunaga's orders (they were suspected of secretly colluding with enemies), Ieyasu chose the latter. During the Warring States era, loyalty could not trump ambition.

When Hideyoshi took over Nobunaga's armies, Ieyasu joined forces with him until Hideyoshi died. Ieyasu had agreed to help Hideyoshi's son, Hideyori, rule. But he eventually fought against the warlords who supported Hideyori and emerged victorious at the decisive Battle of Sekigahara in 1600. Ieyasu then extracted the title of shogun from the emperor in 1603 and turned on Hideyori, who was holed up at Osaka Castle. Ieyasu finally defeated Hideyori and his few allies by attacking Osaka castle, from 1614 to 1615, a siege that ended with Hideyori's death. Richard Cocks, head of the British East India trading company in Japan, recorded in his diary, "They say the taking of this fortress hath cost above 100,000 men's lives on the one part and other, and that on the Prince Hideyori's part no dead man of account is found with his head on, but all cut off.... Neither can the body of Hideyori be found; so that many think he is secretly escaped. But I cannot believe it (June 19, 1615)." His suspicions were correct; Hideyori was captured by the Tokugawa and beheaded along with his eight-year-old son. Ieyasu destroyed the Toyotomi clan shrine, thus ending any possibility of a counterrebellion based on the same strategy that the Minamoto had used against Taira Kiyomori in the late twelfth century. Ieyasu himself died of natural causes in 1616, shortly after the siege, at age seventy-five.

Tokugawa Ieyasu created the last warrior regime in Japan, and his successors ruled as shoguns with few real challenges from the court and lords until the nineteenth century. The shogunate established obligations due from the lords, and expectations from samurai, outlined in a 1615 document titled *Codes for Warrior Households*. Some of the articles in the code continued to emphasize themes found in older warrior precepts, such as studying the civil arts along with military arts, living frugally in accordance with one's station in the military hierarchy, and avoiding frivolous activities like drinking and gambling. For commoners, the shogunate issued constantly changing and sometimes contradictory edicts that defined a variety of crimes. It also had the last word on foreign policy but depended on the lords to conduct international relations on its behalf. Japan's political authority was centered in the city of Edo, but Japan was not centralized. There was neither a national army nor a national tax. Lords ensconced in their domains maintained separate currencies, legal codes, and courts.

Many features associated with the last samurai regime had their roots in the sixteenth century. The main difference between the Tokugawa period and its predecessors was the degree to which those features became more strictly defined during the seventeenth century. During the Warring States period, anyone could be considered a daimyo if he was powerful enough, but from the early seventeenth century onward, a man had to be officially classified as one. The image of the samurai as a relatively strictly defined group distinct from other types of people in Japanese society can be attributed to the Tokugawa period. In earlier times, "warrior" was a plastic concept; some men were born and raised as warriors or served as military vassals or retainers, but others might have been part-time warriors, pursuing other occupations when not at war. In the Tokugawa period, only the lords (daimyo) or shogunate could confer that status.

Hideyoshi initiated a process of pacifying Japan later inherited by the early Tokugawa shoguns and largely complete by the late seventeenth century. He issued an edict known as the *sword hunt* that forbade farmers from owning weapons of any kind and ordered them to hand over weapons to local warrior authorities to be melted down for use in a great Buddha statue. But, as in any premodern society, regulations enacted by the sovereign were never completely and uniformly enforced. Some commoner elites, such as village officials or commoners with warrior roots, still held weapons in secret. Villagers used muskets for hunting, but they were locked up in village headmen's offices and given only to those with written permission from a local authority.

Perhaps Hideyoshi's farthest-reaching act was a countrywide land survey used to determine taxes based on agricultural output. It doubled as a primitive registry. Villages, their residents, and the number of people in a resident's house, including servants, were classified as commoners rather than warriors, thus separating warriors from commoners spatially and economically. But it was only under the Tokugawa shogunate that warriors became distinct from commoners culturally and politically. In general, warriors could no longer live in the countryside except in a few domains where a portion of the samurai population engaged in farming as part of their military obligation. Instead, the shogunate's laws forced samurai to move into castle towns that served as domain capitals, leading to massive urbanization. Edo became the largest city in the early modern world. Merchant activity flowed from the villages into local cities as the Tokugawa population grew. Commoners in the countryside were no doubt glad to see the samurai population leave their villages, but samurai officials made regular forays into the countryside to assess production there.

The shogunate also controlled a third space: the borders between Japan and European countries. Catholic missionaries traveled mostly throughout southern Japan, where nearly a quarter of a million Japanese, some of them warriors, converted to Catholicism. Although these conversions might have been true acts of faith, the reality is that where missionaries traveled, merchants followed. In the sixteenth century, merchant activity increased the wealth for warlords in the south and helped them gather European weapons and ammunition. Of the three warrior hegemons, Oda Nobunaga had nominally accepted Catholicism in Japan, probably as a way to antagonize and weaken his Buddhist institutional rivals. But Hideyoshi and Ieyasu suspected foreigners, their overly zealous and exclusive religious beliefs, and the potentially troublesome southern warlords who hosted them.

Ieyasu's prohibition against Christianity in 1612 was directed primarily at the top. Although the edict outlawed Christianity in general, its implementation targeted lords and samurai converts. This changed in 1637 when rebels in the southwestern region of Shimabara used Catholic imagery—namely, crosses and crucifixes—on their flags during the rebellion. Across Japan, the shogunate required people to join local Buddhist temples to prove that they were not Christian, and authorities forced converts to publicly renounce their faith. The shogun also banned visitors from foreign countries, except from Japan's neighbors, and, oddly, the Dutch—they promised never to bring Catholic-related objects or texts into Japan. Overseas Japanese could not return to Japan, nor could Japanese travel abroad. The shogunate shut down oceangoing ship construction, and all foreign ships had to arrive in Nagasaki, far to the south, far away from Edo. More than just imposing a Catholic ban, the shogunate also wanted to monopolize any foreign contacts, taking away profitable European connections that mostly southern warlords had once developed.

The lords (daimyo)

The first issue facing the early Tokugawa shoguns was how to prevent challenges from the warlords themselves. The shogunate removed many warlords from their bases of power and put them into unfamiliar territory. During the first fifty years of the Tokugawa period, there were at least 281 instances of lords being relocated. A little more than 200 daimyo were completely stripped of land and title, and roughly 170 samurai were promoted to the rank of daimyo. The shogunate awarded another 200 or so lords with more land. It executed particularly threatening enemies, dissolved their domains, and redistributed their land to Tokugawa allies.

The Tokugawa clan existed as a first among equals and maintained a tenuous dominance throughout the Tokugawa period. It controlled sixty thousand warriors and nearly a quarter of the land in Japan, including the area around the major cities of Edo, Kyoto, Osaka, and the sole official international port in

Nagasaki. These lands supplied the shogunate with the resources it needed for mundane operations, including paying its samurai and providing support to the court and emperor in Kyoto. Those same lands funded the shogunate's national responsibilities. When extremist samurai assassinated some Europeans in the nineteenth century, the shogunate had to pay the indemnities to the families. The Tokugawa had their own samurai loyal to them. Most of them served as bureaucrats within the shogunate. The Tokugawa shoguns could not reach into another lord's domain and withdraw men or resources. The samurai in the 250 to 300 domains that existed throughout the Tokugawa period were loyal to their local lord's clan. Although the shogunate could force a daimyo to supply samurai labor for infrastructure projects, such as building dams or bridges, the shogunate could not bypass the lord. It was the lord's responsibility to fulfill the order. If the shogunate needed more samurai to deal with a rebellion or defend against foreign invasion, it would call upon the most loyal daimyo to mobilize their own samurai. The nineteenth century tested the limits of the shogunate's prerogative. Sometimes lords close to the Tokugawa clan answered the call to mobilize against rebels, but when the Tokugawa clan most needed help, some lords demurred, to disastrous effect.

Daimyo staffed all of the top advisory positions in the shogunate, creating a group that, on the one hand, had their destinies tied to the fate of the shogunate. But as lords, they enjoyed relative autonomy in their own independent domains. Theoretically, no lord could have more than one castle, and even repairs to a castle had to be approved by the shogunate to prevent turning a castle "repair" into an expansion. Even Ieyasu's closest allies were not exempt from this rule. One vassal lord who fought with Ieyasu during the Battle of Sekigahara was punished for expanding his castle: the shogunate confiscated 90 percent of his land and sentenced him to home confinement.

With some exceptions, the shogun relied upon the daimyo to interpret the rules as they saw fit, to enforce them as needed, and to mediate relations with Japan's neighbors. Thus, relations with the Koreans to the east, the Ryukyu Kingdom to the south, and the Ezo lands to the north were all managed by daimyo who lived closest to those countries. The lord of Tsushima Island, located between Japan and Korea, acted as a diplomat between the two countries and monopolized Korean–Japanese trade. The shogunate bestowed the rank of daimyo upon the northernmost clan in Japan, the Matsumae, solely because of their role as a go-between for the Tokugawa and the aborigines in Ezo.

But lords had no jurisdiction across domain borders. When a samurai from one domain committed a crime in another domain, only the Tokugawa regime could order the arrest. The shogunate also wanted to prevent neighboring domains from sending troops into one another's territory, which could be the first step in building a regional army used to overthrow the shogunate. This edict had its drawbacks. When the shogunate needed help putting down an insurrection in the south, an event known as the Shimabara Rebellion (1637–38), lords close to the conflict refused to help, fearing that doing so would break the shogunate's rules. Subsequently, the shogunate allowed troops from any domain to cross a border to protect the coasts from invasion or quell insurrection if a domain needed assistance.

To prevent rebellion, the shogunate also wanted to eliminate the age-old practice of using marriage to form strategic alliances. Article eight in the *Codes for Military Houses* explains, "Marriage is the union symbolizing the harmony *of yin* and *yang,* and it cannot be entered into lightly. The Chinese *I-Ching Book of Changes,* says 'Marriage is not to be contracted to create disturbance. Let the longing of male and female for each other be satisfied. . . . To form a factional alliance through marriage is the root of treason.'" Thus, all daimyo marriages had to be approved by the Tokugawa regime.

Early in the Tokugawa period the shoguns enforced rules strictly. To maintain stability in the realm, clans were expected to practice primogeniture; a lord's oldest son, regardless of competency, would become the next daimyo. If a lord did not declare an heir before he died, and if the shogun did not approve the heir himself, then the family lineage could be dissolved and the domain confiscated. Samurai from those domains became "masterless samurai" (*rōnin*) and had to travel to find employment, often ending up in Edo. Complaints from some lords, and the rising problem of masterless samurai causing trouble in Edo, led to the loosening of strict rules beginning in the latter half of the seventeenth century. Thus, while primogeniture was still the norm, lords might delay announcing a son's birth, lie about the birth order of several sons in order to choose a suitable heir, or even postpone announcing the death of a daimyo until the clan's advisors could choose an appropriate successor.

Under a policy of "alternate attendance" (*sankin kōtai*), the shogunate required lords to travel between their home domains and Edo every other year. This practice began as a military expectation, not a requirement. After all, since at least the eleventh century warriors had spent time away from home performing guard duty or some other military service in Kyoto or Kamakura. During the early 1600s, going to Edo to serve the shogun and have an audience with Tokugawa Ieyasu was part of being a close ally. But by the 1640s the practice of alternating time in Edo and the home domain became institutionalized and expected of all lords.

Alternate attendance was rooted in a pre-Tokugawa custom of hostage exchange. Daimyo wives and children lived in Edo permanently to discourage daimyo rebellion. Wives and children were relatively free within the city, but wives were generally forbidden from leaving at all except for pilgrimages to religious sites in the Edo hinterland. In fact, inspectors working at checkpoints along the five official highways that connected Edo to the rest of Japan always monitored samurai women closely. A samurai woman heading away from Edo could indicate the beginning of a rebellion as lords sent their women to safety. For the same reason, travelers heading toward Edo were checked by the inspectors for any guns. Heirs could travel to their domain homeland, but their visits could never overlap with their fathers' presence in the domain—again, to prevent rebellion. Lords expected their teenage heirs to visit the places they would one day rule. But what could attract them to a life in some small, countryside domain? After all, they grew up in the political, commercial, and entertainment capital of Japan. One clan advisor even scolded an heir who, repeatedly citing illness, a common excuse for shirking duties, had refused to visit his domain for many years: "Most daimyo heirs of your status have already made the trip to the domain.... This may lead to rumors that your illness is grave or that there is some discord between you and the lord. People may also be wondering whether you have postponed making the trip to Tosa because you lack the ability to govern."

In addition to keeping a tight leash on the lords' close family, the alternate attendance system drained the lords economically. Even though there was no national tax on the daimyo, the shogunate had ways of extracting economic support from the lords. Daimyo provided funds, labor, and materials to repair the immense Tokugawa castle in Edo and other Tokugawa castles located in other cities, including Kyoto. Lords had to maintain walled compounds in Edo, with a mansion for the family, quarters for full-time servants and guards, barracks for samurai who lived in Edo, stables, training areas, and even gardens. When lords moved back and forth from Edo biennially, they brought with them a retinue of samurai appropriate to the size of the domain as well as a large support staff. Smaller domains might bring only several hundred samurai; larger domains sent several thousand. Edo compounds and the alternate attendance system together composed 50 to 75 percent of a domain's annual budget.

The shogunate coordinated travel so that neighboring lords did not serve in Edo at the same time, perhaps to prevent possible Edo-based collusion between neighbors or to ensure that a lord was always in a particular region in case of uprisings or foreign attack. For the most distant lords, the trip could last several months, and the clan was supposed to pay for food and lodging in the expensive, officially approved inns along the highways. And weather did not always cooperate. Travel back and forth from Edo every other year was a long, burdensome, and costly process. The daimyo were happy to see alternate attendance abandoned when the shogunate weakened and collapsed during the mid-nineteenth century.

Nonetheless, even the strictest laws could be skirted or bent because all of the shogunate's prominent counselors were themselves daimyo and thus sympathized with daimyo burdens. A lord who was busy reforming his domain's finances or otherwise dealing with complex internal political issues could beg off alternate attendance by claiming "illness," the go-to excuse for any samurai bureaucrat desperately seeking a method to protest or skip some duty. A lord required to contribute to a large infrastructure project, such as construction of dams, would also receive a temporary release from alternate attendance. Early in the Tokugawa period, the shogunate expected daimyo to repair Edo Castle, but, in a surprising reversal, the castle went unrepaired while the shogunate sometimes lent money to daimyo to repair their own castles. The shogunate strictly monitored the daimyo in the seventeenth century, but eventually, these inspections became a ritualized affair with few consequences. As long as the lord maintained the appearance of following the shogunate's laws without fail, there were acknowledged workarounds to the daimyo obligations.

Geographically, the most threatening warlords were located far from Edo. A little less than a dozen of the roughly one hundred or so of these "outer" (*tozama*) domains represented some of the largest landholdings in Japan other than those of the Tokugawa clan itself. Many of the outer lords were classified as such because they were not Ieyasu's vassals before 1600. Others received outer daimyo status and were placed far to the south to hem in potentially threatening daimyo. Politically, these *tozama* lords had no access to the decision-making process in the shogunate, but economically they influenced the region around them, especially lords based in the southwest. Some were so powerful, such as the Shimazu clan in the Satsuma domain, that even Tokugawa Ieyasu could not relocate them in the early seventeenth century as he had done to weaker daimyo. Despite the Tokugawa clan's preeminence, it still had to negotiate power with warlords such as the Shimazu in order to solidify its national authority. The oldest and largest outer clans had once been the Tokugawa clan's peers, not subordinates; their claim to power was independent of the Tokugawa. Although the Tokugawa period might have been an era of relative peace, it was not void of tension. Once a year in the Satsuma domain, the samurai dressed in full armor and meditated upon their ancestors' defeat at the Battle of Sekigahara. Warrior mothers in the Chōshū domain told their boys to sleep with their feet facing Edo, an insult to the Tokugawa. For Tokugawa-period samurai, support of, or conflict with, the Tokugawa clan became part of their identity.

The "vassal" (*fudai*) lords served Tokugawa Ieyasu before 1600. Almost half of all lords were vassal daimyo, numbering from just over 100 to a peak of about 130 in the mid-nineteenth century. Some of the most senior vassal lords began as samurai vassals to Ieyasu, men not considered daimyo during the sixteenth century. As the Tokugawa clan and the shogunate expanded, so too did the number of vassal daimyo. Although none of their domains were as large as the largest outer domains, they staffed all of the important offices within the shogunate. Theoretically, the shogunate expected them to serve in times of need; their destiny was tied to that of the shogunate. But they were also potential rivals. Ieyasu confiscated lands from several powerful vassal lords over minor pretexts and even eliminated some clan lines entirely. By the end of the Tokugawa period, however, the title of *vassal* was merely symbolic. It granted a lord the privilege to hold positions in the shogunate but it otherwise guaranteed no special treatment. Many of these daimyo refused to help the shogunate when it attacked rivals in the mid-1860s.

A smaller group of "related" (*shimpan*) lords, never more than around twenty, had kinship ties to the Tokugawa clan itself. The most trusted decision-makers typically came from these families, who were supposed to be the most loyal to the Tokugawa and the shogunate. Their domains were located close enough to Edo to protect it, but not too close—allies and relatives could still be a threat, even in a peaceful era. Some had no landholdings at all. One clan, the Mito, was exempt from alternate attendance and instead resided permanently in Edo. Of these *shimpan* lords, the so-called three houses, the three major branches of the Tokugawa clan, used the Tokugawa surname and supplied heirs to the shogun when one was not otherwise forthcoming.

The samurai life cycle

With some exceptions, birth was the only entrance into the warrior status group. Samurai girls learned how to care for a future husband and his family, while boys learned what it meant to serve the domain, its lord, and his household. Samurai children, even those of modest means, grew up in a household staffed with commoner servants. Families felt pressure to keep up appearances even if they could not afford it. Family planning through abortion or infanticide was a common option for samurai and commoners alike. Health problems compounded a family's financial challenges. Children of both statuses were susceptible to the same diseases, such as smallpox, which could be fatal. Some samurai children, especially those of elite families, faced at least one danger that most commoners did not—lead poisoning. A samurai woman's makeup contained lead that could pass to infants during breastfeeding. In general, commoners also maintained a more diverse diet while samurai suffered from a thiamine deficiency, called beriberi, because they ate too much polished rice and few other grains and little meat. Ironically, commoners who worked in the fields were usually more physically fit as well.

If a samurai boy survived childhood, he passed through several phases marked by changes in clothing and hairstyle until he became an adult, officially, sometime between twelve and sixteen years of age. As with everything else in early modern Japan, there was no uniform approach to samurai education. In general, a boy began his studies around seven years of age outside the home, with tutors and mentors acting as his primary source of early education. Friendships formed at this age were important; childhood peers became colleagues during their adult working life. Mentors and older boys might court a younger boy romantically, even securing permission from the father to establish a relationship. This could blossom into a close platonic friendship in adulthood—though sometimes these affairs became violent.

In the eighteenth century, daimyo started to build domain schools where young samurai studied classical Chinese texts including Confucius's *Analects*, or Japanese military tales such as the *Tale of Heike*, which recounted the war between the Taira and Minamoto families. In addition to basic reading and writing skills, boys learned ethics and what it meant to be a warrior. Not all samurai education was created equal; inequality within the warrior status group began at a young age. In the seventeenth century, boys born into higher-ranking samurai families typically received more education than those at the bottom, but in general, education and literacy rates rose over time.

Not surprisingly, samurai teenagers studied martial arts, either through private training halls (*dōjō*), at a domain school, or a mixture of both. Even martial arts became a source for discrimination among samurai. Only wealthy, higher-ranking samurai might learn how to ride a horse, which was considered a martial art, or study how to shoot from horseback (*yabusame*).

Swordsmanship, however, could be studied by warriors of all stripes. A typical practice session might include engaging in predetermined attack and defense drills (*kata*) with wooden swords and repetition of basic techniques. But lords and high-ranking samurai dominated certain styles, such as Yagyū Shinkage-ryū, the first institutionalized style of swordsmanship. It was named after the Yagyū family, whose headmen taught swordsmanship to the Tokugawa shoguns and received daimyo status for doing so. Like the relationship between artists and shoguns during the Muromachi period (1336–1573), the Yagyū masters met other intellectuals through their connection to the Tokugawa shoguns, and that interaction influenced how swordsmanship was institutionalized and taught. In some domains, samurai students who studied an elite style like Yagyū Shinkage-ryū received a stipend for their equipment and training. They even demonstrated their skills in front of their local lord as part of annual events. Lower-ranking samurai also studied swordsmanship but were limited to lesser-known, newer, or even local styles. Those students often did not receive stipends or permission to perform before their lord. Since these styles did not have as close a connection to warrior officialdom, however, their practitioners could be more creative in how they developed their art—low-ranking samurai engaged in freestyle fencing, the forerunner to the modern sport of kendo.

The shogunate expected samurai to be prepared to mobilize in case of insurrection or invasion, but most samurai had little interest in military training. They rarely practiced beyond their teenage years and, as adults, only attended the occasional mandatory training sessions—Tokugawa samurai had become "sword-wearing bureaucrats." Primarily, samurai used martial arts as a way to connect to their warrior heritage or to interact with men like themselves. They were less concerned about practical application in combat. In many domains, military preparedness was no longer a fact of life. During the latter half of the Tokugawa period, lords no longer required the lowest-ranking samurai to own rifles or carry bows. In fact, martial skills needed to apprehend criminals were considered the lowliest of arts, because samurai rarely conducted physical police-type work. Outcasts and other marginalized commoners hunted down and arrested criminals, guarded prisoners, and tortured and executed offenders.

In adulthood, a Tokugawa samurai's life revolved around his family and the domain. Honor, as far as there was such a notion, was defined by one's conduct and loyalty to the lord's family. Gone were the days of serving a powerful warlord who might have commanded respect by his prowess on the battlefield or his political acuity. The Tokugawa custom of primogeniture did not always guarantee an able or charismatic lord. Thus, samurai worked to uphold the domain's reputation rather than to act out of love for a daimyo. They idealized the legacy passed down from Warring States–era predecessors and honored fictitious ties to famous clans such as the Minamoto or Kyoto nobles like the Fujiwara. A samurai's career trajectory was determined, in order of importance, by the rank of the family, seniority, and talent.

The oldest son typically inherited his father's position. This included a job that might be as menial as guarding one of the gates to the local domain castle for several months out of the year or as important as becoming one of the lord's closest advisors. The situation was worse for younger brothers, who were not guaranteed consistent work by the domain. Since the oldest brother inherited the family property as well, the younger brothers were at his mercy. If they were lucky, they could marry into an heirless warrior family or be adopted by a childless samurai. Otherwise, they had to find some temporary employment or abandon their samurai status. Samurai who tired of searching for menial domain jobs, especially second and third sons, left the samurai life to become scholars, writers, priests, and teachers.

Older scholarship about Tokugawa samurai exaggerated the lack of social mobility within the samurai status. There is a certain intuitive appeal to this argument; warriors before the Tokugawa period could rise through the ranks based on their exploits in war, but in an age of peace, few opportunities existed for a samurai to showcase his talents. Recent scholarship tends to correct past assumptions about samurai inertia. A samurai born into a high-ranking family might begin his career with simple work. As he grew older and demonstrated talent, the domain advisors would give him more responsibility. Low-ranking samurai faced more difficulties rising through those social ranks, but even then, especially when domains faced fiscal or political crises, some could be promoted based on talent alone.

Most rank-and-file samurai were not busy with official duties. Samurai who lived in Edo during their tenure on alternate attendance worked for a few hours every day, and then, with permission from their lord, left the domain compound to go on pilgrimages to Edo-area temples and shrines, essentially a form of sightseeing. Merchants sets up stalls to sell their wares, while street performers and fortune tellers flocked to take advantage of tourists, transforming some temple properties into permanent fairgrounds. Even today, Asakusa Shrine in Tokyo attracts tourists as it did throughout the Tokugawa period. Aside from gambling, drinking, and, if they could afford it, visits to the pleasure quarters like Yoshiwara, samurai studied literature, poetry, music, martial arts, and philosophy alongside commoners or samurai from other domains.

Many samurai supplemented their meager hereditary income with small-scale work. Called *by-employments*, these included micro farming, weaving, pottery-making, trade, and handicraft production (like toys and umbrellas). But not all samurai used their time so nobly. Some of the lowest-ranking samurai gambled, begged, and borrowed their way through life. Katsu Kokichi, a nineteenth-century samurai, recounts his life as a ne'er-do-well in an autobiography written as a warning to his son, the statesman Katsu Kaishū. Kokichi was born the second son of the Otani, an undistinguished samurai family connected to the Tokugawa clan. His father was not a warrior but the third son of a wealthy, blind moneylender who was adopted into the Otani family. He then married into the Katsu family and became its heir. Despite his newly acquired samurai status, Kokichi could not find any steady employment and lived on a meager hereditary stipend, as many lowly samurai did. He eked out a living by renting out a small plot of land, buying and selling swords, begging, stealing, and engaging in other shady activities, some of which landed him in trouble. Like many samurai, he spent much of his life in debt. One samurai writer complained about poor warriors: "They head for guard duty wearing outfits that they have conned the pawnbroker into temporarily restoring to them. Once they have come back from guard duty, they return the outfits directly to the pawnbroker. Their servants mock them for this."

A family history written during the 1930s details similar hardships for a samurai clan from the Mito domain. Despite living hand to mouth, samurai families were under pressure to maintain standards of appearance. As the samurai proverb tells it, "A hungry samurai keeps a toothpick in his mouth even if he has nothing to eat." They had to maintain a certain number of retainers commensurate with the family's rank. In theory, these retainers would join the master of the house during military campaigns, but with war unlikely, this practice became a meaningless custom. Thus, samurai hired commoner men on a temporary basis to accompany them during ceremonial events.

The commoner–samurai gray zone

Did commoners ever dream of becoming samurai? Wealthy rural commoners often used their position and wealth to accrue warrior privileges, such as the right to carry swords or use their surname in official documents. But for the most part, they did not want the drudgery of a low-ranking warrior job. Still, some commoners during the seventeenth century petitioned to receive samurai status. Kian was one such commoner who dreamed of becoming a warrior. His grandmother, the daughter of a samurai, raised him, so he grew up listening to her stories about warriors. As the fourth son of the family, he could not hope to carry on his family's trade, which would pass to his oldest brother. So, in 1655, at age sixteen, he began researching his family's history in order to secure warrior status. He asked neighbors to share documents they had, and he visited the local Buddhist temple to look for old gravestones and records. He eventually abandoned his quest and became the heir to another commoner family, but he still used his research to coauthor a history of the region.

It was rare, but possible, for a commoner to achieve warrior status. An elite commoner could marry into a low-ranking warrior family and become its heir, as Katsu Kokichi's father did. Domain officials granted warrior status to well-known fencing teachers of commoner status in order to employ them as official sword teachers. Wealthy merchants who lent daimyo large sums of money acquired samurai status and worked as economic advisors to the domain. A poor samurai could "sell" his status by officially adopting a commoner as an adult. Often these examples of status crossing were only superficial, used to show off to other commoners, and carried no obligations or offers of actual warrior employment. In any case, a commoner wealthy enough to buy samurai privileges would not desire the lowly, unprofitable work of a samurai.

Complicating the divide between commoners and warriors were those who occupied a gray zone. In many domains, a group of people known by various titles such as "rural samurai" or "landed samurai" lived in the villages and claimed, falsely or otherwise, to have warrior ancestry. They could carry swords or use a surname in an official capacity and represented domain interests in the countryside. In parts of the Kanto region outside of Edo, when wandering gangs of young men caused disorder in the nineteenth century, the shogunate asked landed samurai to establish and train local militias. Daimyo bestowed landed samurai status on rural entrepreneurs for their contributions to the domain, such as bringing new lands into production, which added to the domain's tax base. In Edo, too, entire families known as the "thousand men of the same mind" (*sennin dōshin*), who originally worked as guards during the Warring States period, served as minor officials on the outskirts of Edo. These families interacted socially, often intermarried, and maintained a strong communal identity. Some even trained together in their own style of swordsmanship, Tennen Rishin-ryū, in order to express pride in their warrior ancestry. Shogunate officials sometimes acknowledged them as "warriors"; after all, sennin dōshin worked for the shogunate. At other times, the shogunate revoked their privileges, considering them mere commoners, much to their chagrin.

Despite such warrior–commoner gray zones, samurai writers claimed that no commoner could ever become a true samurai. The most widely read military text of the Tokugawa period, *The Military Mirror of Kai*, stated, "Even if a townsman imitates a samurai his heart is still that of a merchant. In the heat of battle he would worry about losing his property. He lacks the essence of bushido and would not be of any use." In this case, the term *bushido* does not refer to an institutionalized "code" of behavior for the samurai, as no such code existed. It simply indicated the fundamental difference between samurai and commoners: a samurai was born into his status and performed whatever duties were expected of him, even if that work overlapped with commoner occupations. Other than paying taxes and providing corvée labor, a commoner had no such intimate ties to the warrior regime. For more than 260 years, the warrior regime kept nonsamurai out of its decision-making process while also attempting to limit, often unsuccessfully, what commoners could do in their daily lives. It is no wonder that most people, even some samurai, were glad to see warrior authority collapse.

Chapter 5
Inventing the samurai

It might seem that an invisible wall separates samurai and nonsamurai, and, thus, we think of their inherent differences: samurai could wear two swords and use surnames whereas commoners could not; samurai resided in the castle towns while peasants lived far away in the countryside. Commoner–warrior relations were often antagonistic. Commoners had to pay taxes to the warrior regime, and warriors, in theory, could cut down a commoner if he insulted a samurai, a practice referred to as a "disrespect killing" (*burei uchi*). As generalizations, these might be true sometimes. Records indicate that in one domain a disrespect killing occurred about once every four years. But rather than trace the differences and antagonisms between samurai and commoners, we should consider their similarities. If the age of the samurai began during the Tokugawa period, then so too did the modern idealized image of Japanese warriors.

In establishing the samurai as a distinct social group, the shoguns unwittingly created an idealized image of the samurai that was available for consumption by commoners as well. The samurai might have numbered no more than 8 percent of the national population, but the invention of samurai identity during the Tokugawa era penetrated commoner culture. Commoners imitated, celebrated, parodied, and criticized samurai. When swordsmanship became a social activity to help create bonds among samurai men, wealthy commoner men wanted to participate. Manuals that taught samurai men how to conduct themselves in a romantic relationship with their juniors became popular among wealthy merchants, too. Even kabuki theater, the exemplar of urban culture, associated with red-light districts, commoners, and gaudy presentation, existed in Edo City, initially, as theater performed mostly in daimyo compounds for a warrior audience.

The collapse of the last samurai regime is often explained in terms of domestic political upheavals, economic woe, and foreign pressure. But at least some of the decline can be explained by the recognition among samurai and commoners that an irreconcilable gap existed between samurai ideals and samurai reality, a gap that had been widening throughout the Tokugawa period.

Even the most mundane features of samurai life became a source of fascination for commoners. The most widely read text in Tokugawa Japan was the "warrior roster" (*bukan*). Published several times a year, it listed details of all the daimyo in Japan and most of the prominent samurai working in the shogunate. It included family crests, clan lineage, addresses, gifts received from and given to the shogun, the distance from a lord's compound to Edo Castle, and the positions samurai held in the Tokugawa regime. Samurai needed to know who their colleagues and superiors were within the Tokugawa bureaucracy, especially because jobs constantly changed. But the quantity of rosters published suggests that commoners purchased them even more than samurai. Commoners in big cities like Edo, Osaka, or Kyoto, where the rosters were sold, needed these details to serve their samurai customers. Identifying a samurai crest during a daimyo procession or knowing where to deliver products was part of doing business. But possessing and updating the rosters for free at a bookstore several times a year by having new pages pasted in was much like the excitement of obtaining the latest baseball roster in the modern world. In other words, commoners enjoyed access to information about warriors that had been unavailable to them before the seventeenth century.

The simple act of publishing information about samurai and daimyo differentiated Tokugawa-era warriors from their predecessors. This process had roots in an earlier era when warrior identity was defined through texts. Elite, literate warriors in the fifteenth and sixteenth centuries learned warrior culture through etiquette manuals (*kojitsu*) that described appropriate behavior such as how to dress during ceremonies or to conduct oneself during an archery competition. Warrior customs and rituals dated back to the Kamakura period but applied mostly to the housemen who lived in or frequented Kamakura city itself. Writings about warrior culture in general increased during the Muromachi period, when warriors and nobility interacted with greater frequency and royal culture influenced warrior thought. Etiquette manuals from that time continued to be popular during the Tokugawa period, but the rosters did more than simply trace the contours of elite warrior culture. They defined exactly what made warriors important. Moreover, they created a degree of occupational uniformity that had not existed much before the seventeenth century.

Newly installed lords and elite warriors took seriously the pressure to define themselves. Many unemployed samurai (*rōnin*), who had been left adrift in the aftermath of the Warring States period, found work as teachers and advisors to daimyo in Edo and castle towns throughout Japan. These masterless samurai helped families plan and participate in warrior ceremonies that increasingly became part of warrior social life, especially in Edo. Minor lords had to create genealogies in order to foster clan identity where previously there had been none. Wandering samurai also published military histories and military science books, such as the early Tokugawa-era text *Military Mirror of Kai*, whose author, Obata Kagenori, became a sought-after teacher of military science.

Warrior ideals

Commoners were exposed to warrior values through popular culture. In Edo, kabuki began as theater for largely warrior audiences, and as such, plays celebrated warrior heroes and values. After kabuki opened to the masses, the Edo dandy replaced the warrior as the archetypal hero, but even he was depicted as embodying warrior traits such as bravery, martial prowess, and loyalty.

The most frequently performed kabuki play was called *The Treasury of Loyal Retainers*, also known as the *Akō Incident* or the *47 Rōnin*. It appeared first as a puppet play based on a historical event that occurred in the early eighteenth century when a daimyo named Asano attacked a senior shogunate samurai, Kira, during a ceremony within the shogun's castle. It is unclear why Asano assaulted Kira, but it is commonly believed that Kira insulted Asano for not knowing proper etiquette. Kira, a master of ceremony for nearly forty years, was in charge of ensuring that all attendees knew their roles, including the much younger, small-domain-holding Asano.

Since drawing a sword in the shogun's castle was forbidden, shogunate police immediately arrested Asano, "executed" him by *seppuku* (ritual suicide by disembowelment and decapitation performed by a trusted colleague, if one was lucky), and dissolved his Akō domain, forcing his retainers to become masterless samurai (rōnin). After nearly two years of planning to avenge their lord's death, forty-six of the forty-seven rōnin attacked and killed Kira. Some contemporaries argued that the rōnin hoped to avoid harsh punishment because their actions reflected loyalty to their lord. Instead, they were sentenced to seppuku. Earlier warrior regimes had no single form of capital punishment, nor did pre-Tokugawa-era samurai disembowel themselves often. But Tokugawa-era samurai idealized seppuku as warrior machismo of a bygone time, going as far as writing manuals standardizing the ritual. The Tokugawa shogunate established seppuku as capital punishment.

Although the incident itself passed with little comment when it first occurred, audiences loved the dramatized versions. The attack and mass ritualized suicide made for dramatic scenes. Moreover, these were lowly samurai acting in unison against authorities and sacrificing themselves as a group, a theme that might have appealed to urban commoners who often interacted with low-ranking warriors.

On the one hand, the historical event and its subsequent popularity represented a crisis for Tokugawa samurai because it exposed the tension between warrior ideals and warrior reality. Samurai, as men of action, were supposed to display loyalty to their lord's clan and domain. They celebrated past warrior heroes and their bravado. On the other hand, samurai were no longer supposed to be violent. The shogunate attempted to prevent war at the top, among daimyo, through rules for daimyo activity such as expanding castles, pursuing warrior crimes across borders, and the like. It also forbade samurai from engaging in fights and punishing offenders with execution. Samurai writers promoted Confucian learning and self-cultivation, not violence, as admirable traits. In other words, how could a samurai think of himself as a warrior in a world with no warfare and without being violent? That tension was never fully resolved during the Tokugawa period, and samurai pundits did not agree on any one image of the ideal samurai.

Some samurai writers praised the forty-seven rōnin because they acted out of a personal sense of loyalty to their lord. Others argued that the rōnin had acted improperly because it was not Kira who killed their lord; the shogunate executed Asano for his criminal offense—the shogunate's law trumped personal notions of action, honor, and loyalty. One writer criticized them for waiting more than a year to carry out an attack when they should have killed

Kira immediately after Asano's execution. Hayashi Hōkō, head of the Confucian academy in Edo, synthesized the two views, citing classic Chinese texts to explain the heart of being a warrior.

> First I will view their vendetta from the perspective of the hearts of the forty-six men. It was imperative that they "not share the same sky with their master's enemy" and that they "sleep on reeds, using their sword as a pillow" [both quotations from the Chinese *Record of Rites*]. To hang onto life by enduring shame and humiliation is not the way of the samurai. We must also consider the vendetta from the perspective of the law. Anyone who sees the law as his enemy must be put to death.... These two perspectives are hardly identical, but they might complement each other in operation, without contradiction. Above, there must be humane rulers and wise ministers who govern by clarifying law and promulgating decrees. Below, there must be loyal retainers and righteous samurai who readily vent their anger in the determined pursuit of their cause.

The eighteenth-century book *In the Shadow of Leaves* (*Hagakure*) contains the most extreme reaction to the bind between the violent legacy of warriors and their pacification. Tokugawa warriors would, in theory, be executed for fighting each other regardless of the reason. So what should a samurai do if he is insulted by another samurai, especially a lower-ranking one? He could be executed and his family punished if he attacked the offender. But if he ignored the slight, he risked losing face in front of his warrior peers. The answer, according to Yamamoto, the book's author, was to choose death. Yamamoto had his own opinion of the forty-seven rōnin—they should have killed Kira immediately without worrying about their fate. Dishonor was worse than the death of an individual samurai because his death is singular while dishonor can spread to his family and, more importantly, could affect the reputation of his lord's clan. The *Hagakure*'s opening line, "The way of the samurai is in death," and his criticism of local samurai and the shogunate made it quite controversial. It circulated privately among samurai in the Nabeshima domain and was generally unknown until its resurrection as propaganda during the height of war and fascism during the 1930s.

Within the Tokugawa world, violence was no longer appropriate samurai behavior. Though cultivating the self by studying the Chinese classics like *The Analects* was part of warrior learning before the seventeenth century, Tokugawa samurai values relied on later Chinese interpretations of those ancient texts, a school of thought called Neo-Confucianism. Neo-Confucianism informed Tokugawa samurai attitudes toward lord, family, and society. "Cultured" learning (*bun*) should still be tempered with training in martial learning (*bu*), argued warrior leaders, but there were no longer opportunities to display one's martial prowess other than within the confines of martial arts practice. Martial arts had become nothing more than the physical manifestation of *bun*-focused cultivation.

These values did not square with the reality of most samurai who, like Katsu Kokichi, worried about basic survival. And if they had at least some pretension of wealth, they were more interested in pursuing extracurricular activities. The putative golden age of samurai identity always existed in an idealized past. As one samurai commentator complained in 1818, "In past ages, it was common for warriors to mock those who pursue elegance as 'courtiers.' Now, though, it is the better warriors who behave like courtiers; the majority have become like women."

Samurai writers connected this "spiritual" impoverishment to economic decline, and they often blamed urbanization for the stain of commoner fashions on warrior lifestyle. One intellectual chastised warriors in Edo for spending money "as if living in an inn." By being forced to move back into the countryside, samurai would be allowed to return to a self-sufficient lifestyle, live a simpler life, and relearn the "purer" warrior values reminiscent of an earlier age. Others noted that urban commoners would follow samurai to the countryside and focus on farming rather than working for the large samurai populations in castle towns.

Beginning in the eighteenth century, the shogunate enacted a series of reforms to address the twin problems of samurai economic distress and declining samurai identity. Matsudaira Sadanobu, the grandson of the eighth Tokugawa shogun, a senior advisor in the shogunate and the architect of late eighteenth-century reforms, envisioned a Confucian-styled society based on order, with the morally superior gentlemen warriors firmly at the top. The reform included edicts that tried to censor publications, curtail merchant activity, and eliminate heterodox teachings. But he was particularly interested in cutting shogunate expenses and demanded that samurai practice frugality and focus on developing their *bun* and *bu*. He too idealized the rural origins of the samurai and took his own samurai retainers on hikes in the countryside.

Despite the warrior authorities' attempts to reinvigorate samurai identity and behavior, samurai themselves poked fun at the image. A well-known satirical response to Sadanobu's reform went, "*Bun bu, bun bu*, I can't sleep at night!" Many of these writers, who came from low-ranking samurai families, abandoned dead-end careers for intellectual pursuits. One such man was Hiraga Gennai, a teacher, writer, and inventor who lampooned the stuffy samurai image in an essay titled "On Farting" (1771) about a performer who excelled at farting as a musical talent. Gennai used a country bumpkin samurai named "Crankshaw Stonington, Esquire," as the straight man to critique warrior values. Crankshaw admonished the fartist and the crowd, telling them that the shogunate allowed street performances in order to teach the public about fealty and loyalty; he cited the forty-seven rōnin incident depicted in the *Treasury of Loyalty Retainers* as an example. "Flatulence," he added, "is, after all, a personal matter and should not be aired in public. Any proper samurai would be mortified to the point of suicide if he were inadvertently to let, uh, fly in polite company." Gennai's critique illustrates how commoners appropriated culture in their own ways, even as the shogunate tried to promote warrior values via popular culture. He also mocked the notion of samurai honor—even a harmless fart could push a samurai to commit suicide rather than risk public shame.

Samurai parody frequently appeared in popular literature as well. The Tokugawa period's most famous novel, *Shank's Mare*, written by the son of a minor warrior, recounts the adventures of two men, Kita and Yaji, who drink, play, and bumble their way from Kyoto to Edo. In a roadside bar the two encounter a drunk samurai, a few young women (one of them named Shime), and a buffoon:

> "Oh, you horrid man," cried the girls. "Look at his face. Look what strange eyes he makes. How bright and glaring they are!"
>
> "You are insulting," cried the samurai, in a sudden burst of anger. "Look at your own faces instead of mine..." He stood up, but the waitresses caught hold of him. "There, There," they said. "There's nothing for you to get angry about."
>
> "Don't be rude, Shime," said the buffoon. "I'll tell you what we'll do. We're getting rather bored, so to liven things up, let's be as jolly as if we were in a steam bath."
>
> "A steam bath is an empty bath," said the samurai. "He takes me for an idiot. I've a good mind to beat him for his rudeness." Apparently the samurai was an angry drunk.

The samurai summoned the girls and the buffoon to entertain him for the evening, but in the end, he tried to reinforce the notion that nonsamurai should know their proper place when interacting with a samurai, twice accusing them of rudeness. But rather than cower from him, they continued to tease him, knowing that his drunkenness and futile attempts to lord his status over them only made him seem powerless.

9. The artist Hokusai, best known for his "Great Wave" woodblock print, pokes fun at the warrior sense of duty. Here three retainers wait close by, unwavering, as their master smells up the outhouse.

Writers and artists understood that bodily functions were the same across class divides, and they used bathroom humor to critique any group, especially samurai, that put on airs. The artist Hokusai, famous for his "Great Wave" woodblock print, published a book of prints containing a scene titled "Privy," which depicts samurai retainers standing dutifully by while their superior relieves himself. The three retainers believe in the samurai ideals all too much, sacrificing their own comfort in the name of duty.

Commoners and warrior identity

Unlike their pre-Tokugawa counterparts, commoners helped create warrior culture. They purchased warrior rosters, studied swordsmanship, hired warrior tutors, and bought military-related books. They celebrated samurai ideals in popular culture, both in rural areas and in the cities. Villagers in the countryside organized kabuki plays that featured battle scenes with large casts that incorporated members of local youth associations. Quite simply, war plays broke the monotony of everyday life. Some commoners even studied martial arts not only for self-defense and as a way to rub elbows with samurai but also to use the techniques in rural theater and village festivals.

To a certain extent, samurai writers promoted commoner participation in warrior culture. Commoners either read or listened to public recitations of a fourteenth-century war tale called *The Chronicle of Great Peace* (*Taiheiki*). The *Taiheiki* recounted the conflict between the northern and southern courts in that era. The authors glorified Emperor Go-Daigo's general Kusunoki Masashige and celebrated values such as loyalty and self-sacrifice. As an educational text, it taught young commoners how to read Chinese characters (*kanji*) and imparted moral lessons. The *Taiheiki* was so well known that authors used it as a historical setting to comment on politically sensitive events—the forty-seven rōnin incident, for example—rather than risk arrest for writing about taboo topics.

Other pre–Tokugawa period warrior texts circulated among commoners and samurai. Books like *A Woman's Imagawa* and *A Commoner's Imagawa* copied themes found in the fifteenth-century "Imagawa Letter," a widely read letter of advice to warriors, and emphasized the importance of cultured learning (*bun*). Of course, not all peasants could read, but some village headmen lectured to villagers about morals using the same military writings popular among samurai.

The shogunate alternatively forbade and encouraged the most martial of samurai activities, namely, swordsmanship and archery. Consider the following 1805 edict from the shogunate that circulated throughout the nineteenth century in many domains surrounding Edo:

> We have heard that in this region there are unemployed samurai wandering about. Peasants are learning martial arts and gathering together for practice which might cause them to ignore their agricultural work. They forget their status and become uppity. They should be told to stop and martial art instructors should not introduce their arts to the villagers.

The edict introduces several issues facing warrior authorities during the nineteenth century. It begins by illustrating samurai unemployment. *Rōnin* who were desperate to make a living ignored shogunal decrees that prohibited them from making warrior culture available to commoners. By providing samurai culture to commoners in the form of martial arts instruction or tutoring, they unintentionally recognized its universal appeal and applicability to anyone who could afford it. Wealth, not birth, could buy at least some warrior fantasy. Commoners had eclipsed warriors as an economic force even though warriors controlled the land. Sadanobu's reforms and the ones that followed it failed to solve the decline of samurai identity and economic woe. The edict also demonstrates that the regime could not prevent commoners from appropriating warrior culture in their own way. Whether commoners were emulating or parodying them, samurai did not control how they were perceived or how they were portrayed.

As economic and social disorder spread throughout the greater Edo region during the mid-nineteenth century, the shogunate began to rely on commoners to provide self-defense. Its Kantō Regulatory Patrol, created to deal with rising criminality in the Edo hinterland, depended on rural elites for information about local criminals. Villages joined together to form defense leagues. They were organized by larger, wealthier villages that hosted criminal holding centers. The village headmen received privileges typically reserved for samurai—the right to wear swords and use surnames in official documents. League members practiced swordsmanship for its practical use and to strengthen internal social cohesion.

The increasing presence of Westerners in the seas around Japan exposed many structural weaknesses of warrior rule. Officials in Edo were so worried that the imperial Ise Shrine was vulnerable to Westerners that after an 1855 inspection, they asked the Shinto priests to survey temple bells that could be melted down to be used for cannons and rifles and to start training commoners in martial arts, especially gunnery, as a first step toward local defense against invasion. This effort culminated in 1863 when the shrine formed a peasant militia. Peasant militias became more common in the mid-nineteenth century as foreign and domestic threats were too much for the shogunate to contain with warriors alone. Warrior reality, it seems, could not match the heroic feats enacted on stage, in books, and in the fencing academies.

Collapse and "restoration"

There were many problems that led to the Meiji Restoration (1868), a conflict between samurai led by *tozama* daimyo who fought in the name of the teenage Meiji emperor and the Tokugawa shogunate and its allies. Although it was not as large a war as the US Civil War, it nonetheless has the status of being the mythic "origin" of modern Japan. In the decades before the Restoration, several interconnected problems squeezed the samurai regime and warriors in general: the threat from Western countries, strife within the shogunate itself, and the changing relationship between samurai and nonsamurai. These pressures originated in the early seventeenth century at the latest and arose from policies enacted by the warrior regime to maintain samurai hegemony.

By the early nineteenth century, leaders in the shogunate worried about how to address the growing presence of Westerners on the edges of Japan. In 1825, as more European ships tested Japan's waters, coastal daimyo were ordered to fire on those ships to drive them away, an effort that was largely unsuccessful. The shogunate eventually abandoned that order, but it illustrates the shogunate's inability to adequately prepare for foreign threats. More American whaling ships in the Pacific and increasing trade in China led to a rising number of shipwrecked sailors in Japan. The British, French, Dutch, and Russians had been trying to expand commercial access and diplomatic relations throughout Asia, and the shogunate did not want to fall prey, as the Chinese had done during the Opium Wars (1839–42), to a series of conflicts over Britain's opium trafficking in China. To some warriors, the Europeans were nothing more than opportunistic merchants, an occupation that samurai deemed selfish and lowly. But these warriors believed that if they could contain foreign merchant activity to Nagasaki, they could avoid diplomatic entanglements. Unlike in Europe, trade among East Asian countries at the time did not presuppose any diplomatic relations between governments. During the latter half of the eighteenth century, after repeated attempts by Russians to open relations to Japan, the shogunate allowed them to conduct minor trade in Nagasaki, hoping that this would mollify them. It did not, and a Russian captain landed on Tsushima Island in 1861 and demanded that the daimyo there lease him land. Unable to scare the Russians off, the shogunate had to ask the British for help.

Western pressure culminated with the arrival of US admiral Matthew Perry in Edo Bay in 1853. The shogunate had heard from the Dutch and the Ryukyu kingdom that Perry was on his way, but the appearance of his "black ships" so close to Edo instead of Nagasaki caused a panic within the shogunate's leadership. Many samurai were benignly curious rather than deeply perturbed. Warrior officials and American ship personnel peacefully examined each other's weapons. Nonetheless, Perry's demand that the shogunate respond to President Millard Fillmore's request to establish at least limited trade and diplomatic exchange, if not an outright treaty, affected the shogunate's relationship to both the daimyo and the imperial institution.

Perry promised to return in a year's time with better-armed ships. In the interim, the chief senior advisor in the shogunate, Abe Masahiro, broke Tokugawa precedent by asking all of the daimyo, including those from the outer domains who were typically shut out of the formal decision-making process in the shogunate, for their opinions on how to respond to the Americans. Why, after a little over two hundred years of keeping them at political arm's length, would the shogunate need their voice?

The answer to that question connects to an issue that all prominent warrior families had faced since at least the beginning of the Kamakura period, and possibly earlier—the problem of succession. The Tokugawa shogun at the time, Ieyoshi, died only weeks after Perry arrived the first time, and his successor, Iesada, was weak politically and physically, having suffered from several diseases since childhood. Abe and his supporters controlled the shogunate's policies but did not do so with impunity. He needed consensus because the shogunate was weak.

Unfortunately for Abe, a consensus was not forthcoming. Daimyo response ranged from some form of "opening the country" to the Americans by engaging in trade and learning from their science and technology to an insistence that all American requests be rejected, even if doing so risked an unwinnable war. When Perry returned in 1854, Abe signed the Treaty of Kanagawa. Neither he nor the daimyo who supported a treaty embraced the West per se. The treaty did not guarantee the Americans much, and Japan avoided war, but criticism from many daimyo, politically influential nobles in Kyoto, and samurai loyalists to the emperor and its institution was swift and powerful.

When studying the Tokugawa shogunate, it is easy to forget about the other perennial issue in samurai history: every regime's interaction with the court and emperor in Kyoto. The Kyoto nobility did not influence political and social events in Tokugawa Japan to the same degree it did before the seventeenth century. The nobility and emperors remained in Kyoto, and few Japanese knew or cared about them. People encountered royalty only in history writing. But because history writing is always done with an agenda, whether the author knows it or not, people understood the imperial institution through the lens of samurai authors. Historical works published throughout the Tokugawa period had to assess Go-Daigo's Kenmu Restoration of 1333. Was his southern court the legitimate imperial line that had been wronged? Was Ashikaga Takauji a rebel who acted against the imperial institution or an admirable leader who was justified in creating a new shogunate once Go-Daigo's leadership had descended into chaos? Was Takauji to be demonized or celebrated? And what did the answers to those questions mean for warrior legitimacy as it related to the supposed divine lineage of the emperors? No single view dominated, but when Kyoto residents awoke on a late winter morning in 1863 to find the decapitated heads of three Ashikaga shoguns pilloried along the Kamo River, clearly the pro-emperor views had gained currency as never before. The accompanying placard labeled "vengeance of heaven" portended bad things to come for the shogunate. Heaven, in this act, sided with the imperial institution and not with the Ashikaga shoguns who inherited Takauji's legacy.

The Tokugawa period was the apex of warrior dominance in Japanese history and especially shogunal authority over the court. Political dominance should not be understood as a complete lack of political influence for the court, however. Respect for the emperor and the imperial legacy spread among the samurai in the latter half of the Tokugawa era, in part as a result of history writing.

In the seventeenth century, the Mito domain, led by a daimyo family tied to the Tokugawa clan itself, began an immense history-writing project titled *The Great History of Japan*; it was completed in 1906. As with much scholarly work in Japan before the twentieth century, the text was influenced by Chinese thought, in this case, Neo-Confucianism. It also followed Chinese historical style by tracing change over time through the descent of the emperor. Samurai teachers used the content as teaching materials, and its focus on the emperors influenced several generations of samurai who took seriously the twin themes of loyalty and imperial prestige. By the time Perry arrived, writers who had followed a wide range of schools of thought, from ancient Chinese learning to nativist teachings about Japan, and even those who dedicated their lives to studying imported European texts, had been convincing many that the Tokugawa clan and its shogunate ruled only at the behest of imperial grace.

Newfound respect for the imperial institution connected to foreign policy, with disastrous results. In 1846, an imperial rescript commanded the shogunate to build coastal defenses. In 1858, the emperor rejected the shogunate's attempt to seek after-the-fact approval for a commercial treaty it signed with the United States. Criticisms leveled against the shogunate by nobles, daimyo, samurai, and even some commoners culminated in unprecedented violence. In 1860, a group of rōnin from the Mito domain descended upon a senior councilor's entourage as it approached Edo Castle. They killed the guards, who had their swords tucked in the scabbards to protect against the snow, and assassinated the councilor, Ii Naosuke, still in his palanquin. Throughout the 1860s, samurai from across Japan, mostly low-ranking, underemployed men, left their domains for Kyoto to gather around the court and like-minded loyalist samurai. Meanwhile, the shogunate tried its best to pursue détente with Kyoto and its supporters, arranging a marriage between the emperor's daughter and a shogun. It also dutifully answered a summons from the court to send the shogun to Kyoto in 1863, illustrating the extent to which the warrior regime had lost its control of the emperor. Humiliated and unable to deny the emperor's command, the shogunate promised to follow an imperial order it could not keep. The shogun, in his ancient role as the general who would "expel the barbarians," agreed to force Europeans out of Japan.

While many daimyo played little role in the Kyoto-shogunate politics and did not feel directly affected by Westerners, they still faced pressure from commoners in their domains. Unlike other revolutions in world history, Japan did not experience a revolutionary movement among commoners. Peasants complained about tax hardships and the bad behavior of local officials, but they never attacked the basic structure of the daimyo–shogunate warrior regime. They drew on the Confucian concept of benevolence to plead for leniency, and if they did not receive it, they could protest. It was a risky strategy, and ringleaders were often executed, sometimes alongside their family members, children included. The most desperate villages sent men to Edo to appeal directly to the shogun himself as he traveled through the city in a covered palanquin. But it was a tactic that could work. In the best-case scenario, the shogunate would investigate a troubled area and force the daimyo to make reforms. At the very least, a protest illustrated daimyo incompetence and could lead to ridicule and punishment, such as confiscating the domain and putting another daimyo in charge.

Villagers could collectively pressure their daimyo, but merchant groups could yank purse strings. Wealthy merchants and rural entrepreneurs held sway over some rank-and-file samurai and in some cases even had access to daimyo. As moneylenders, they could advise daimyo how to enact economic reforms within the domain. Daimyo often looked to commoners to expand industries that would bring more income and tax revenue into the domain. Among middle-ranking samurai who drew their stipends and other resources from villages assigned to them in the countryside, several employed villagers in their mansions in Edo or followed demands that the family change its spendthrift ways or be cut off from future loans. And when Japan's economy encountered global capitalism, merchants in big cities profited from textile trade with Europeans. Trade was so successful that prices of goods skyrocketed throughout the 1860s, and these increases led to riots and "smashings" against warehouses where the wealthy were accused of hoarding goods. Among the many imperial loyalists were commoners, women included, who felt that they too should play a role, no matter how minor, in the future direction of Japan.

The mystique and majesty of warrior rule had dwindled by the 1860s, and those who believed in warrior notions of loyalty, obligation, and action started uprisings around Japan. They attacked what they saw as the most offensive representatives in the shogunate, such as Ii Naosuke, and enemies within their home domains and among the nobility in Kyoto. Factionalism in some domains resulted in small-scale civil wars, numbering hundreds of men on each side, in large outer domains in the south and in the smaller but politically connected domain closer to Edo.

Not a single year during the 1860s passed without some degree of political violence. The era before that decade had been relatively calm, but now the peace was destabilized by factionalism and domain civil wars, attacks against Europeans and their servants living in newly formed merchant communities in Yokohama, riots in the cities of Kyoto and Edo, and the unexpected deaths of two key political figures, the shogun Iemochi (in 1866, at age twenty) and the emperor Kōmei (1867, at age thirty-five). The new emperor, Meiji, was only a teenager and was controlled by a handful of court nobles and their daimyo supporters. The new shogun, Yoshinobu, was a reluctant successor. Not wanting to start a war with his enemies at court and no doubt fearing for his life, he "returned" the title of shogun to the emperor in 1867, setting up the "restoration" of political rule to the Meiji emperor in name, if not in reality. Yoshinobu remained the head of the Tokugawa clan, a partner with the court and emperor, and leader of the samurai bureaucrats attached to the shogunate. He mounted an attack against daimyo gathered at Kyoto who he claimed were manipulating the young emperor. His army of fifteen thousand troops outnumbered those from the southwestern domains, but the battle at the villages of Toba and Fushimi on the outskirts of Kyoto did not go his way. He retreated to Edo and surrendered the Tokugawa forces to the emperor in 1868.

Despite Yoshinobu's surrender, supporters of the Tokugawa clan, including a few French military attachés, continued to fight against the southern daimyo and their soldiers who composed the "emperor's army." The samurai holdouts did not fight out of love for the shogunate; indeed, when a few thousand men commandeered the shogunate's ships and left for Hakodate in the north, they created a republic and installed a Tokugawa family member as its president. Another thirty-eight domains in the northeast formed a military alliance to fight against the fifty thousand troops sent under the emperor's banner from the south.

For the first time since the early seventeenth century, tens of thousands of troops were being mobilized for war, but they were hardly like their predecessors. Long before the war, the shogunate had been reforming its military, arming it with Western rifles and asking the French for help reorganizing its tactics. In the south, the British and other western Europeans had been selling rifles left over from the American Civil War. Daimyo there formed "peasant" militias to help in coastal defense, although it was mostly samurai who were dispatched to fight in the emperor's name. Still, traditional weapons like swords, spears, halberds, and bows appeared on the battlefield.

The bloodiest fighting occurred in the northeast Aizu domain, ruled by the Matsudaira clan. Despite having been given up by the Matsudaira as a hostage, Ieyasu never completely abandoned them. Branch lines of the Matsudaira clan formed after Ieyasu's death celebrated the older Matsudaira–Ieyasu connection, and they remained among the most reliable supporters of the shogunate even as it fell two and a half centuries later. While Aizu samurai bore the brunt of the siege against Aizu Castle, their women inside took care of the wounded, tried to supply food, and packed gunpowder and ammunition in makeshift bamboo bazookas; when cannonballs landed on the roof, women covered them with wet blankets to keep them from setting fires. Although the men implored them not to, samurai women eventually joined them in battle with swords and halberds, the first people to use them in combat since at least the sixteenth century. Many women cut their hair to look like men, and one even donned her dead brother's clothes. In the end, nearly 200 women died in the fighting. Another 230 old men, women, and children committed suicide lest they suffer dishonor at the hands of their enemies. Years later, the Aizu domain's house elder Saigō Tanomu recounted the suicide of all the women in his family: his mother, wife, younger sister, and five daughters, the youngest of whom were four and two. Each wrote a death poem. His thirteen-year-old daughter wrote, "If you take my hand / and we go together / I won't get lost," to which her sixteen-year-old sister added, "When the time comes, I will take it / as we depart for death on the mountain road."

10. This woodblock print by Tsukioka Yoshitoshi reflects his experience as a witness to the violence of the Meiji Restoration as it unfolded in Ueno. Although the words on the 1868 print describe the life of Komagine Hachibei, a rebel fighting during the seventeenth-century Shimabara Rebellion, the clothing style clearly reflects the dress of a Shogitai member. The Shogitai was one of many groups of irregulars who fought on the side of the Tokugawa shogunate.

Post-Restoration warrior legacy

In 1872, only a few years after the Meiji Restoration, a southern ex-samurai turned modern oligarch named Itō Hirobumi delivered a speech in San Francisco. He stated, with a disregard for history, that despite a temporary civil war, the feudal system had been destroyed without "firing a gun or shedding a drop of blood." History textbooks in Japan from the late nineteenth century to the present tend to downplay the violence of the Restoration. One prominent historian in Japan went so far as to suggest that the Meiji Restoration was a unique revolution in world history because it involved relatively little violence compared to other modern revolutions and that the samurai abolished their own class. During a short presentation on the need to reconsider the violent and traumatic nature of the Meiji Restoration, this same historian, sitting in the audience, argued that local tourist boosters had been responsible for overemphasizing Restoration violence only long after the fact. He might be right, but that still does not erase the deaths of more than thirteen thousand people killed during the latter half of the 1860s, most of them during the Boshin War that began after Yoshinobu's capitulation and ended in 1869. Such is the controversy of the Meiji Restoration even 150 years later: not even the dead are given their due.

The Meiji Restoration ushered in a sweeping abolition of the shogunate, the nearly 280 extant domains, and warrior status itself. The newly formed Meiji oligarchy first asked the lords to voluntarily "return" their domains to the emperor, effectively eliminating them. Prominent daimyo with large domains who led the Restoration forfeited their domains first. Later, the government forced all daimyo to do so. Some were moved across the country to become governors in one of the seventy-two newly formed prefectures, but many were not. For the most part, daimyo did not bemoan their new status. They received payoffs that ensured them a comfortable retirement. Even before the

Restoration, a few daimyo had asked the shogunate to take control of their domains, as continuing to try to govern them had simply not been worth the effort.

Samurai response to the end of the status system was mixed. The newly formed government replaced the traditional samurai stipend with bonds that were immediately bought back by the national banks. Some lower-ranking samurai profited nicely from this transaction and used the cash to establish factories and businesses. For higher-ranking samurai, however, the stipend–bond switch fell short of providing a decent living.

Moreover, the physical vestiges of samurai privileges were eliminated; samurai could no longer carry swords or maintain their distinctive hairstyle. And they no longer monopolized the military, which was now open to all males. Ex-samurai in the government enacted these laws, but even within the bureaucracy there were widely contrary opinions. In 1869, one such official in the newly formed deliberative assembly proposed that swords no longer be carried in public by anyone but police, military, and government officials. He was dismissed from the assembly, demoted in rank, and threatened with death. This same assembly spent more time debating whether or not to abolish seppuku than on how to interact with Western countries—it voted against eliminating seppuku by 200 to 3, and the man who proposed the idea was assassinated.

With their status abolished, many samurai could not find jobs that utilized their backgrounds. Nor were they trained to handle money; being above financial dealings had been a source of pride during the Tokugawa period, a field of knowledge relegated to selfish merchants. Some former warriors were so impoverished that they sold the swords, armor, and other samurai objects that now fill Western museums, selling family heirlooms just to survive. Others were happy to be free from the bounds of their previous status, now able to pursue whatever occupation pleased them. A granddaughter of a samurai who later published a history of her family states that her grandfather, a samurai of the Mito domain, was glad to see the old system fall. He found it was easier to make a living even though he, like all samurai, lost his traditional stipend.

Far from celebrating the samurai, many Japanese in the late nineteenth century considered the samurai an anachronistic embarrassment, unproductive, and useless. Instead, a vogue for all things Western, even dress, spread throughout society. Local governments destroyed their abandoned castles. In the Aizu domain, the newly formed prefectural government sold off the land surrounding the castle, where much of the fighting had occurred. They opened the structure to local tourists for a twenty-day viewing before tearing it down and auctioning the materials. Only one person made a bid. The land around the castle was sold off to local farmers.

But by the end of the nineteenth century, samurai represented the putative strength of a unique, traditional Japan. The most famous ex-samurai turned modern intellectual, Fukuzawa Yukichi, who is featured on the 10,000-yen bill, is well known for celebrating the end of the status system and the Tokugawa shogunate. Nonetheless, he later bemoaned the disappearance of the samurai spirit represented by the "losers" of the Meiji Restoration, such as the Aizu fallen and the Tokugawa shogunate's samurai. For their part, many of those losers now worked in the Meiji oligarchy, and the Aizu men, once regarded as hated enemies of the emperor, found newfound respect from those who celebrated Japan as a martial country.

As Japan embarked on wars against China (1894–95) and Russia (1904–5), ideologues promoted the notion that now all Japanese were samurai. Kendo, a modern form of swordsmanship that used armor and point scoring, was introduced into the school system because it fostered martial spirit. Self-sacrifice and love of the emperor became a central theme in literature, film, and primary school textbooks. *Hagakure*, once a marginal text at best, was republished in the early twentieth century and enjoyed a wide readership, especially during the 1930s, at the height of Japanese fascism.

And what of the "way of the samurai?" It was not nearly as influential among the populace as it was among government officials and high-ranking military men. Most people credit Nitobe Inazō for defining *bushido* for a modern audience in his book *Bushido: The Soul of Japan*, published in 1900 in English for Americans. But nearly a decade before Nitobe, a journalist and politician, Ozaki Yukio, described bushido as Japan's version of gentlemanliness, comparable to Europe's notion of chivalry. His concept said nothing of martial prowess or self-sacrifice. Throughout the 1890s, intellectuals responded to Ozaki's writings about bushido. Some used the word to describe the vitality of commerce or argued for a Christian version of bushido, but no single definition dominated until the twentieth century. Nitobe had been living in the United States during the first bushido boom in Japan, and when his book was published in Japanese, it barely registered among anyone except interested intellectuals who deemed it too little too late. Instead, the philosopher Inoue Tetsujirō popularized the concept of bushido as a repository for nationalism, service to the emperor, and self-sacrifice. Those themes, and samurai history in general, became central to World War II propaganda. Samurai appeared in textbooks, boys learned Japanese fencing at school, and girls practiced how to wield a glaive (*naginata*), a long staff with a curved blade attached to the end.

After the Second World War, this wartime samurai image was taboo. Samurai films, a popular genre even during the silent film era, were censored by the American occupation army. Directors could still make samurai films, but they could not glorify violence, self-sacrifice, or loyalty to the emperor. A samurai film boom occurred during the 1950s after the occupation ended, when classic films such as Akira Kurosawa's *Seven Samurai* appeared, but they no longer portrayed an ultranationalist version of the samurai. The US occupation forces also banned martial arts practice, which was seen as another vehicle for disseminating dangerous bushido and fascist ideology. Even when martial arts like kendo reemerged, they emphasized cooperation and competition and deemphasized martial applicability.

During the high economic growth beginning in the 1960s, the archetypical, dark-suited "salaryman" became the new samurai. Called the "corporate warrior," such a businessman remained loyal to his company and would never abandon it for a better deal elsewhere—unlike a medieval warrior who readily switched sides or betrayed his lord. As for self-sacrifice, it was the exception that proved the rule of self-preservation for early warriors, but the business samurai was expected to sacrifice his well-being for the company. One wonders how the use of a more historically accurate image of the samurai might affect Japanese culture, business, and politics in the future.

References

Chapter 1

Bonnie Rochman, "Samurai Mind Training for Modern American Warriors," *Time*, September 6, 2009.

Yamamoto Tsunetomo, *Hagakure*, trans. Alexander Bennett (Tokyo: Tuttle, 2014), 60.

Chapter 2

For a full English translation of the law code, see David Lu, *Japan: A Documentary History* (Armonk, NY: M. E. Sharpe, 1997), 1:109–15.

Statement from Japan's 1869 government: Margaret Mehl, *History and the State in Nineteenth-Century Japan* (New York: St. Martin's Press, 1998), 1.

Chapter 3

Peter D. Shapinsky, *Lords of the Sea* (Ann Arbor: Center for Japanese Studies, University of Michigan, 2014), 6, 106.

David Lu, ed., *Sources of Japanese History* (Armonk, NY: M. E. Sharpe, 2015), 1:153–54.

Obata Kagenori, *Kōyō Gunkan jo*, ed. Koshihara Tetsurō (Tokyo: Kyōikusha, 1979), 40:69.

Donald Keene, *Yoshimasa* (New York: Columbia University Press, 2006), 15–22.

Hōjō Sōun letter: Translation my own. For alternative translation of full text, see Carl Steenstrup, "The Imagawa Letter," *Monumenta Nipponica* 28, no. 3 (Autumn 1973): 299–315.

Twenty-One Articles: Translation my own. For full version of alternative translation, see Carl Steenstrup, "Hojo Soun's Twenty-One Articles," *Monumenta Nipponica* 29, no. 3 (Autumn 1974): 283–303.

Chapter 4

Richard Cocks diary: This version from Constantine Vapori, *Voices of Early Modern Japan* (London: Taylor & Francis, 2018), 63.

Relocation of lords: Harold Bolitho, *Treasures among Men: The Fudai Daimyo in Tokugawa Japan* (New Haven, CT: Yale University Press, 1974), 8.

Advisor scolds heir: Constantine Vaporis, *Tour of Duty* (Honolulu: University of Hawai'i Press, 2016), 19.

Insults to Tokugawa: Albert Craig, *Choshu in the Meiji Restoration* (Cambridge, MA: Harvard University Press, 1961), 22.

Sumurai complains about poor warriors: Buyō Inshi, *Lust, Commerce, and Corruption* (New York: Columbia University Press, 2014), 56.

Kian dreamed of becoming a warrior: Yoshida, *Hei to nō no bunri* (Tokyo: Yamakawa Shuppansha, 2008), 97–101.

Chapter 5

Hayashi Hōkō explains the heart of being warrior: Quoted in part from *Sources of Japanese Tradition*, vol. 2, part 1, *1600–1868* (Armonk, NY: M. E. Sharpe, 1997), 361.

Buyō Inshi, *Lust, Commerce, and Corruption* (New York: Columbia University Press, 2014), 43.

Jippensha Ikku and Thomas Satchell, trans., *Shank's Mare* (Boston: Tuttle, 1960), 339.

Saitamaken, *Shinpen Saitamaken-shi Shiryōhen* (Urawa, Japan: Saitamaken, 1979), 742–43.

Translated by Anne Walthall in *Politics and Society in Japan's Meiji Restoration: A Brief History with Documents* (Boston: Bedford St. Martin's Press, 2017), 141.

Further reading

General history

Friday, Karl, ed. *Japan Emerging: Premodern History to 1850*. New York: Routledge, 2012.

Hane, Mikiso, and Louis G. Perez. *Premodern Japan: A Historical Survey*. Boulder, CO: Westview, 2015.

Warrior origins

Farris, William W. *Heavenly Warriors: The Evolution of Japan's Military, 500–1300*. Cambridge, MA: Harvard University Press, 2010.

Friday, Karl F. *The First Samurai: The Life and Legend of the Warrior Rebel Taira Masakado*. Hoboken, NJ: Wiley, 2008.

Early warrior authority

Friday, Karl F. *Hired Swords: The Rise of Private Warrior Power in Early Japan*. Stanford, CA: Stanford University Press, 1996.

Lu, David J. *Japan: A Documentary History*. Armonk, NY: M. E. Sharpe, 2005.

Mass, Jeffrey P. *Antiquity and Anachronism in Japanese History*. Stanford, CA: Stanford University Press, 1995.

Mass, Jeffrey P. *Yoritomo and the Founding of the First Bakufu: The Origins of Dual Government in Japan*. Stanford, CA: Stanford University Press, 1999.

Mass, Jeffrey P., and Takeuchi Rizo. *The Kamakura Bakufu: A Study in Documents*. Stanford, CA: Stanford University Press, 1976.
Oyler, Elizabeth. *Swords, Oaths, and Prophetic Visions: Authoring Warrior Rule in Medieval Japan*. Honolulu: University of Hawai'i Press, 2006.

War and culture

Berry, Mary E. *The Culture of Civil War in Kyoto*. Berkeley: University of California Press, 1997.
Berry, Mary E. *Hideyoshi*. Cambridge, MA: Council on East Asian Studies, Harvard University, 1990.
Conlan, Thomas. *State of War: The Violent Order of Fourteenth-Century Japan*. Ann Arbor: Center for Japanese Studies, University of Michigan, 2004.
Friday, Karl. *Samurai, Warfare and the State in Early Medieval Japan*. New York: Taylor & Francis, 2005.
Ōta, Gyūichi, trans. *The Chronicle of Lord Nobunaga*. Edited by J. S. A. Elisonas and Jeroen Pieter Lamers. Leiden: Brill, 2011.
Shapinsky, Peter D. *Lords of the Sea: Pirates, Violence, and Commerce in Late Medieval Japan*. Ann Arbor: Center for Japanese Studies, University of Michigan, 2014.

Warriors: Late sixteenth to mid-nineteenth centuries

Bolitho, Harold. *Treasures among Men: The Fudai Daimyo in Tokugawa Japan*. New Haven, CT: Yale University Press, 1974.
Hanley, Susan B. *Everyday Things in Premodern Japan: The Hidden Legacy of Material Culture*. Berkeley: University of California Press, 1997.
Katsu, Kokichi, and Teruko Craig. *Musui's Story: The Autobiography of a Tokugawa Samurai*. Tucson: University of Arizona Press, 2003.
Totman, Conrad D. *Early Modern Japan*. Berkeley: University of California Press, 1995.
Vaporis, Constantine N. *Tour of Duty: Samurai, Military Service in Edo, and the Culture of Early Modern Japan*. Honolulu: University of Hawai'i Press, 2016.
Yamakawa, Kikue. *Women of the Mito Domain: Recollections of Samurai Family Life*. Translated by Kate W. Nakai. Stanford, CA: Stanford University Press, 2001.

Warrior myth and legacy

Benesch, Oleg. *Inventing the Way of the Samurai*. New York: Oxford University Press, 2016.

Buyō, Inshi, Mark Teeuwen, Kate Wildman Nakai, Noah Arlow, and John Breen, trans. and eds. *Lust, Commerce, and Corruption: An Account of What I Have Seen and Heard, by an Edo Samurai*. New York: Columbia University Press, 2017.

Goro, Shiba, and Teruko Craig, trans. *Remembering Aizu: The Testament of Shiba Goro*. Ishimitsu Mahita, Honolulu: University of Hawai'i Press, 1999.

Jaundrill, D. C. From *Samurai to Soldier: Remaking Military Service in Nineteenth-Century Japan*. Ithaca, NY: Cornell University Press, 2016.

Index